Things That Matter Most

by

John H. Jowett

(1864-1923)

Published 2014 by Classic Domain Publishing

ISBN-13: 978-1500703202

ISBN-10: 1500703206

Note From The Editor Of Classic Domain Publishing:

In Matthew 22:37-40 Jesus re-emphasized what was repeatedly written in the Old Testament:

" 'Love the Lord your God with all your heart and with all your soul and with all your mind.' This is the first and greatest commandment. And the second is like it: 'Love your neighbor as yourself.' All the Law and the Prophets hang on these two commandments."

It is obvious that these are the most important of all commandments. And, as Jesus emphasized, all the Law and all that the Prophets have these two most important commandments as their foundation. It helps of course to have details and examples on how to accomplish these two commandments "that matter most."

Our love of God must be sincere, not in word and tongue only. Not only should our love of affection be given to God, but also all the powers of the soul and mind must be engaged for him and ever ready to hear and carry out His commandments. Likewise to love our neighbour as ourselves, is the second great commandment.

There is a selfishness (or self-love) which is corrupt, and the root of many sins – it must be put off and mortified. But there is a self-love that is proper – as we must have a due concern for the welfare of our own souls and bodies. Also it helps in understanding what others need. And so we must love our neighbour as truly and sincerely as we love ourselves. In many cases we must deny ourselves for the good of others. By these two commandments – if followed will mature you into what God wants you to be.

About The Author

From Christian Classics Ethereal Library:

John Henry Jowett was one of the most beloved preachers of the early 20th century. His sermons boasted a fine balance of practicality, expressiveness, and depth of knowledge; Jowett had a rare ability to relate to almost every congregant from his pulpit. The 1907 issue of British Weekly, after surveying its readership, ranked Jowett as Britain's "most appealing preacher," over and above even F.B. Meyer, G. Campbell Morgan, and others. In 1913, Jowett published "Things That Matter Most", a collection of short devotionals. "In these days of incessant movement," his preface reads, it serves us well "that we have interludes when the soul can correct her conscious and unconscious wanderings by the contemplation of the serene and majestic things of God." Meditating on sin, grace, redemption, and developing the Christian life, "Things That Matter Most" gives readers a place to pause and listen for God's voice.

THINGS THAT MATTER MOST

Devotional Papers

by

John H. Jowett, D.D.

(1864-1923)

PREFACE

I HAVE ventured to call these devotional papers by the general title, "Things That Matter Most," for, although they are concerned with many themes, I think that in every instance, we come face to face with some supreme interest of the soul. The mountains are never below the horizon: they are always in sight, and they dominate the plains.

It is surely well in these days of incessant movement, movement which so frequently means strain rather than strength, that we have interludes when the soul can correct her conscious and unconscious wanderings by the contemplation of the serene and majestic things of God. It is in the ministry of these interludes that these meditations are now published, and I heartily hope that in this way they may be helpful to those who read them.

J. H. J.

NEW YORK.

THINGS THAT MATTER MOST

TABLE OF CONTENTS

I. THE ILLIMITABLE LOVE OF GOD

WHAT is the biggest thing on which the human mind can be exercised? In what can we most easily lose ourselves in the overwhelming sense of the immeasurable? There are the vast lone spaces of the stellar fields, peopled with countless worlds, crossed by mysterious highways, with stars as the pilgrims, ever moving on their unknown journeyings. We can lose ourselves there. There is "the dark backward and abysm of time," opening door after door in ever-receding epochs, back through twilight and dawn into the primeval darkness, where the inquisitive mind falters and faints. And we can lose ourselves there. There is the appalling wilderness of human need, beginning from my own life, with its taint of blood, its defect of faculty, its dreary gap in circumstance and condition, and repeated in every other life in every street, in every city and village and country throughout the inhabited world. And we can lose ourselves there. And then there is the deadly, ubiquitous presence of human sin, in all its chameleon forms--well-dressed, ill-dressed, blazing in passion, mincing in vanity, and freezing in moral indifference and unbelief. All these are stupendous themes, and the mind that ventures upon them is like the dove that ventured upon the waste of waters, and, soon growing weary of wing, returned to the place of its rest. But there is something more majestic than the heavens, more wonderful than the far, mysterious vistas of time, more pervasive than human need, and more abounding than human sin. The biggest thing with which the mind can cope is the infinite love of God; and all our sanctified powers, and all the ministries of holy fellowship, and all the explorations of eternity will never reach a limit in its unsearchable wealth. The biggest thing you and I will ever know is the love of God in Jesus Christ our Lord. There will always be "a region beyond," and for the already wondering eyes there will always be a new surprise: "The height, and depth, and length, and breadth, and to know the love of God, which passeth knowledge."

8

1. Let us reverently gaze into the height of the love of God. In love the scale of height is measured by the degree of purity. The height in the scale of diamonds is determined by an analogous standard. A diamond is of the "first water" when it is without flaw or tint of any kind. And love is lofty in proportion to its brilliance. Love can be deteriorated and degraded by the tint of jealousy. It can be debased by the tint of envy. It can be vulgarized by a strain of carnal passion. These earthly elements may be mixed with the heavenly substance, and its spiritual value is reduced. So that the first test to apply to any love is the test of purity, which is the test of height, the test as to how far it is sublimated, and separated from selfish and fleshly ingredients which dim and spoil its lustre.

Now it is here that the Scriptures begin in their revelation of the love of God. They begin with its brilliance, its holiness. "In Him is no darkness at all!" How would that be as a description of a diamond? "No darkness at all!" Nothing sinful in His love! But more than that. Nothing shady in it, nothing questionable: nothing compromising or morally indifferent! No darkness at all; no blackness of faithlessness; no twilight of forgetfulness; "no night there!"

And thus it is that, when the Book guides us in the contemplation of the eternal love, it first of all leads us into the contemplation of the eternal light. Always and everywhere this is where we begin. If I listen to a psalmist, he leads me into the holy place: "Exalt the Lord our God, and worship at His holy hill; for the Lord our God is holy." If I listen to a prophet, I am led into the same sacred precincts: "The high and lofty One whose name is holy." If I listen to the mystic seraphim of the Old Testament, I hear them cry one to another, "Holy, holy, holy is the Lord of Hosts." If I listen to the songs of the Apocalypse, I find them burdened with the same theme: "They rest not day and night saying, Holy, holy, holy, Lord God Almighty." If I reverently listen to the Master in His secret communion with the Unseen, I hear Him say, "Holy Father." And if I listen to the prayer which He Himself teaches me to pray, I am led immediately to the holy glory of the Lord: "Our Father . . . hallowed be Thy name." Always and everywhere this is the beginning of our contemplation. We are led away into the light, into the unshadowed brilliance, into the holiness of God. If, therefore, God's love be symbolized by a mountain, its heights will be clothed in the dazzling whiteness of the everlasting snow. Love's heights are found in love's holiness. "God is light," "God is truth," "God is love."

From this primary teaching I wish to adduce two inferences. And the first is this. The force of love always depends upon its height. We find the analogy in water. The force of falling water is determined by its height. In an English home, if your shower-bath is lazy and loitering, chilling you rather than bracing you, your remedy is to raise your cistern, and in the increased height you will get the requisite tingle. The tonic is born in loftiness. It is even so with love. There is a type of love which has no vigour because it has no height. It is a weak, sickly sentiment which just crawls about you. It is low, and therefore it has no enlivening force. It is mixed with earthly elements, and therefore it has no heavenly quickening. It enervates, it does not invigorate. The more holy love is, the higher it is, and the more fraught it is with vitality. How, then, must it be with the love of God? Born in holiness, it has power enough to waken the dead. Have you seen an Alpine river, born amid the snows, and rolling gloriously through the vale? That is the figure we need: "And I saw a river of water of life, clear as crystal," proceeding from "the great white throne," out of the unshadowed depths of eternal holiness. "There is a river the streams whereof shall make glad the city of God," and the holy power of that river is determined by the holy heights in which it is born.

And the second inference is this, that the ultimate ministry and goal of love is also determined by the height of its holiness. Once again seek your analogy in water. Water rises no higher than its source. Water can lift no higher than its source. It is even so with love. Our love can never raise a

10

loved one higher than the love itself. There are aspects of that law which are altogether staggering. Take the love of a parent for his child. Our own tainted love will not lift our child into purity. Our own jealous love will not lift our child into an unembittered disposition. Our own envious love will not lift our child into moral serenity. Our love will not lift above its own level. That is the solemn responsibility of a lover, that if the love be low it will scarcely lift the beloved one above the plains. If we want to lift higher we must heighten our love. How, then, is it with the love of God? His love, so glorious in holiness, can raise to its own level, and lift us into "heavenly places in Christ Jesus." "They shall sit with Me on My throne." "God so loved the world that He gave His only begotten Son, that whosoever believeth on Him should not perish, but have everlasting life." God's love imparts its own loveliness, until one day we too shall be "altogether lovely."

From the supreme height of the fells, on the island of Arran, there comes rolling down the granite slopes a gloriously alive and vitalizing stream. They call it "The White Water," and it is well named. It gleams on the slopes like the whitest foam. Out at sea, when everything else was obscure, I could see the white water running on its ceaseless errand. And oh! the loveliness of its bequests, and the unutterable beauty of its dells and glens! It feeds the bracken, it nourishes the stalwart heather, it moistens the retiring fern. The White Water endows its haunts with its own loveliness. And the white water of the eternal love, ceaselessly flowing from the holy heart of God, brings with it power to make everything lovely, and at last to present everything spotless before the throne.

2. Let us gaze into its depths. Let me link together detached sentences from the Word, that in their associations we may discern what is meant by the depth of the love of God. "The high and lofty one whose tame is holy." . . . "He is gone to be guest with a man that is a sinner!" "Jesus, knowing that the Father had given all things into His hands, and that He was come from God, and went to God . . . began to wash the disciples' feet." "And

one cried with another, saying, Holy, holy, holy is the Lord!" . . . "Neither do I condemn thee; go, and sin no more!" All these are suggestive of what is meant by the love-depths of our God. And on these I want to build this teaching, that it is only the really lofty that can truly reach the really deep. The arm that can reach far upward is the only arm that can reach far downward. It is only holy love that can deal with humanity's deepest needs. A low love has no depths of service. Low love is a thing of compromise, and has no dealings with extremes, whether of holiness or of sin. Pharisaic love had no height. "I thank Thee I am not as other men are." That is not loftiness: it is superciliousness; it is not the vision from the snow-white hills. And because Pharisaic love had no height, it had no corresponding depth; and when the Pharisee saw One descending into the deep pits of human need, he cried in self-respecting amazement, "He eateth and drinketh with publicans and sinners!" Holy love, crystalline love, goes down and down into human necessity, and is not afraid of the taint. Sunbeams can move among sewage and catch no defilement. The brilliant, holy love of God ministers in the deepest depths of human need.

God's love is deeper than human sorrow, and how deep that is my appointed lot gives me daily and deepening experience. But drop your plummet-line into the deepest sea of sorrow, and at the end of all your soundings "underneath are the everlasting arms." God's love is deeper than death, and there are multitudes who know how deep grim death can be. "Just twelve months ago," said a near friend of mine a week or two ago, "I dug a deep grave!" Aye, and I know it was deep enough. But the grave-digger's spade cannot get beneath our Father's love. God's love is deeper than the deepest grave you ever dug! "And entering into the sepulchre they saw an angel," and you can never dig into any dreary, dreary dwelling of death which is beyond the reach of those white-robed messengers of eternal love. Yes, God's love is deeper than death. "O death, where is thy sting? O grave, where is thy victory?"

And God's love is deeper than sin. One night, when I was recently crossing the Atlantic, an officer of our boat told me that we had just passed over the spot where the Titanic went down. And I thought of all that life and wreckage beyond the power of man to recover and redeem. And I thought of the great bed of the deep sea, with all its held treasure, too far down for man to reach and restore. "Too far down!" And then I thought of all the human wreckage engulfed and sunk in oceanic depths of nameless sin. Too far gone! For what? Too far down! For what? Not too far down for the love of God! Listen to this: "He descended into hell," and He will descend again if you are there. "If I make my bed in hell, Thou art there." "Where sin abounded, grace did much more abound." "He bore our sin"; then He got beneath it; down to it and beneath it; and there is no human wreckage, lying in the ooze of the deepest sea of iniquity, that His deep love cannot reach and redeem. What a Gospel! However far down, God's love can get beneath it!

Stronger His love than death or hell,

Its riches are unsearchable:

The first-born sons of light

Desire in vain its depths to see,

They cannot tell the mystery,

The length, and breadth, and height!

3. Let us gaze into its breadth. Here again. I want to say that the breadth of love is determined by its height. Low love is always very confined and exclusive. Lofty love is liberal and expansive. Low love is like a lake; lofty love is like a river. We can imprison a lake within our own estate; we cannot imprison a river. It will be out, and about, and on! And sometimes we foolishly try to imprison the love of God. "We make His love too narrow by false limits of our own." Men have tried to appoint social limits, and national limits, and ecclesiastical limits, and credal limits. We may as well

try to break up the sea into allotments as to "peg out" the love of God. The love of God is as broad as the race, and nowhere is there a single man in any clime, or of any colour, in congested city, in tropical jungle, or on a lonely frontier-line where a pioneer has built himself a primitive home-- nowhere is there a single man, woman, or child who is orphaned of a place in the eternal Father's heart. "If He lose one He goeth out!" . . . O love of God, how broad!

4. And what of its length? There is no end to it. To what length will it not go? "Greater love hath no man than this, that a man lay down his life for his friends." To that length! "Becoming obedient unto death, even the death of the cross!" To that length! "Goeth after that which is lost until He find it." To that length! God's love is as long as the longest road. God's love is as long as the longest day. God's love is as long as the longest night. God's love is as long as life. God's love is as long as eternity. "I have loved thee with an everlasting love." "I will never leave thee nor forsake thee." "Love never faileth."

II. LOVERS OF GOD

I WANT to guide the thoughts of my readers to the soul's love for the Lord, and the fitting words must be pure as light and simple as childhood. Not that the subject is simple. There is no subject more delicate, more intangible, more elusive. It is ever the simplicities that most easily evade our intellectual grasp. What more simple than the love of a little child, and yet how spiritual, and therefore how infinite! And so it is when we come to a theme like the soul's love for our God. We feel awkward and clumsy, as if we were dealing with tender and sacred refinements, and we lack the requisite softness of hand and foot. We have not the delicacy of soul for approaching the exquisitely shy and retiring genius; and even if we see her beauties and her manners afar off, we have no fitting speech wherewith to describe her charms. For themes of this kind require not only very rare and special powers of vision, they require an almost equally rare and unique vocabulary. If we are going to speak about the love of the saints, those to whom we speak must not be made to gather like students in a herbalist's museum; they must feel as if they were out in the sunshine, among all sweet and natural things, amid enticing perfumes and lovely hues. They must not be as though they were studying the laws of physics in the classroom, but as though they were basking in the cheery heat rays of the enlivening sun. In our time there have been two men who could move about this field of the soul's love with the incomparable ease of master-lovers--Spurgeon and Newman, and I always repair to them when I want to put a bit of edge on my own sadly blunt and ineffective blade. Both were deeply intimate with the delicate ways of the soul, and with the love-songs of the soul; so much so that when they began to speak about it the warm, luscious words and phrases of the Song of Solomon became their spontaneous ministers of expression.

The dictionary cannot help us in our quest. The dictionary attempts its definition, but when the definition has been given we feel it is a birdless cage, and the sweet, living songster is not there. Here is what the dictionary says: "Love, an affection of the mind excited by qualities in an object which are capable of communicating pleasure." There you have it! But does any young lover or old lover recognize the withered thing? It is not only withered--it is imperfect and broken. I think we must admit that definitions do not take us very far. To try to put love in a phrase is like taking a bit of tender seaweed out of the water; it becomes featureless mush in the hand.

When I turn to the New Testament no definition of love is given. Everywhere there are signs of love's presence, and she is always engaged in ennobling and beautifying service. Her works are manifest, but the worker herself is elusive. Where she moves there is indescribable energy; there are powerful ministries of purity, and diverse experiences are drilled to a common and beneficent end. Everywhere wildernesses become gardens, and deserts are rejoicing and blossoming as the rose. But one thing is said, and said very clearly, and it is this--the way to love our fellows is by becoming lovers of God. "The first of all commandments is, Thou shalt love the Lord thy God." Everywhere this is taught--love for God is the secret of a large, beneficent, and receptive humanity. How, then, can we become "lovers of God"?

First of all, we must consort with the God we desire to love. We must bring our minds to bear upon Him. Love is not born where there has been no communion. There must be association and fellowship. I know that there is "love at first sight." Yes, at a glance the soul leaps to its other half, and completes a union appointed in the deep purpose of God. And I know there is "love at first sight" with Christ. It is even so with multitudes of little children. It is even so with older people; the road of their life has suddenly swerved, circumstances have brought their souls to a new angle, and there He stood, and their soul was in love with Him! But even this first-sight love needs the sustenance of careful communion. That is just what so many of us deny our souls. We do not give ourselves time. We must bring back something of the quietness of the cloisters into our own turbulent life. We must recover something of the seclusion of the monastery, the ministry of fruitful solitude. We must make space to contemplate the glory of the Lord, and especially those characteristics of the Divine life which are fitted to constrain our souls into strong and tender devotion. Says St. Francis: "The death and passion of our Lord is the gentlest and, at the same time, the strongest motive which can animate our hearts in this mortal life; and it is quite true that the mystical bees make their most excellent honey in the wounds of the lion of the tribe of Judah, who was killed, shattered, and rent on Calvary. . . . Mount Calvary is the mount of Divine love." But the communion must be wider than this. Let me give another quotation from another of the old mystics: "Have the Lord devoutly before the eyes of your mind, in His behaviour and in His ways, as when He is with His disciples, and when He is with sinners, . . . setting forth, to thyself in thy heart His ways and His doings; how humbly He bore Himself among men, how tenderly among His disciples, how pitiful He was to the poor, how He despised none nor shrank from them, not even from the leper; how patient under insult; how compassionate He was to the afflicted; how He despised not sinners; how patient He was of toil and of want." But our meditation upon these high things must be real meditation, the meditation that deepens into contemplation, and absorbs and possesses the glory. Our souls must gaze upon the glory until something of the sense of sacred ownership steals upon them. Political economists have recently been saying very much about "the magic of property." The phrase suggests the new and deeper interest we have in things when they become our very own. And when we begin to even faintly realize that God has given Himself to us, and we can truly and reverently use the words "Our Father," "Our Saviour," life becomes the home of wondrous joy and inspiration. "He loved me, and gave Himself for me."

And, in the second place, we must consort with them that are lovers already. It is well that this should be through personal intercourse, if such happy privilege come our way. But if this immediate fellowship be denied us, let us seek their company through the blessed communion of books. Let me name one or two of these great lovers of God, and quote a few of the love phrases by which they describe their high communion. Let us make friends with John Woolman, and hear his speech laden with phrases of this kind: "A motion of love," a "fresh and heavenly opening," "the enlargement of gospel love," "a love clothes me while I write which is superior to all expression," "the heart-tendering friendship of the Lord," "the descendings of the heavenly dew." And let us make friends with Samuel Rutherford. I might quote nearly everything he has written. Let this suffice: "Christ enquired not, When He began to love me, whether I was fair or black. . . . He loved me before the time I knew; but now I have the flower of His love; His love is come to a fair bloom; like a young rose opened up out of the green leaves, and it casteth a strong and fragrant smell." "If I had vessels I might fill them; but my old, riven, and running-out dish, even when I am at the well, can bring little away. . . . How little of the sea can a child carry in its hand! As little do I take away of my great sea, my boundless and running-over Christ Jesus." Would it not be a good thing for us to drop some of our reading to spend an hour in communions like these? And then let us seek the company of Andrew Bonar: "I felt something of that word," "my soul longeth, yea, even fainteth," "and I lay down this night intensely desiring to feel constrained by the love of Christ." "I have been getting remarkable glimpses of Divine love in answer to earnest prayer that I might know the love that passeth knowledge." And I feel I must give my readers a little extract from one of this great lover's prayers: "As we get into the enjoyment of Thy love may we find that we need scarcely any other heaven, either here or hereafter, only more of this love and the continuance of it." And we must make friends with Horace Bushnell, a man of the most masculine intellect, and yet with one of the tenderest hearts I know in devotional literature. Read these words, written on the shores of Lake Waramaug, in the evening of his life: "The question has not been whether I could somehow get nearer--nearer, my God, to Thee; but as if He had come out Himself just near enough, and left me nothing but to stand still and see the salvation; no excitement, no stress, but an amazing beatific tranquillity. I never thought I could possess God so completely." "God comes to me--so great, benignant, pure, and radiant. What a wonder is God! What a glory for us to possess Him! "Is there any wonder that these were among his last words: "Well now, I am going home, and I say, the Lord be with you, and sin grace, and peace, and love; and that is the way I have come along home."

There are many other great lovers whose names might have been mentioned, and whose friendship it would be well for us to cultivate. The doors of their hearts are always open, and their fellowship is always ready. But these will suffice. Let me mention a third method by which we shall be helped to become lovers of God. I think we ought to sing the songs of the great lovers, songs that will create and nurse kindred dispositions in ourselves. I mean songs of this kind: "O love that will not let me go"; "O love of God, how strong and true"; "Jesus, the very thought of Thee"; "Jesus, Thou joy of loving hearts"; "Let all men know that all men move under a canopy of love." Songs of this loveful, soaring kind will lift our souls to heaven's gate. The ministry of the lovers' songs is not fully appreciated in the Christian life or they would more frequently be upon our lips. Bird trainers train their little choristers to sing through the medium of other birds whose song is rich and full. And we, too, can train ourselves to become lovers of God by singing the songs of those whose love is passionate and matured.

III. FORGETTING GOD

THERE is one word of God which runs through the Scriptures like a sad and poignant refrain, "My people have forgotten Me." "Forgotten" is an intense and awful word. It surely expresses the final issue in human alienation from the Divine. Open and deliberate revolt against God shows, at any rate, some respect to His power. And even formal prayer, empty though it be, offers some recognition of God's existence. But to forget Him, to live and plan and work as though He were not, to dismiss Him as insignificant--this is surely the last expression of a separated life. People are never really dead so long as they are remembered. The real death is to be forgotten. How, then, do we come to forget God? In what sort of conditions is this appalling forgetfulness brought about? I wish to quote two or three descriptive words from the Scriptures in which I think some of these cases are described.

"Afraid of a man that shall die, and forgettest the Lord thy Maker." The fear of man destroys the nobler fear of God. I suppose that one may say that two commanding fears cannot occupy the soul at one and the same time. One fear can drive out another. The fear that is created by the cracking of a whip can drive out the fear which possesses a shying horse when he sees some unfamiliar object upon the road. If a fire break out on a cold wintry night, the fear of the flames can drive out of the soul the fear of the frost. It seems as though one fear draws to itself the energies of the mind, and other fears are left with no sustenance. A big tree in a garden-bed sucks into its fibres the juices of the soil for many yards around, and other growths are starved, and they wither and die.

So it is with "the fear of man." It drains to itself the mental energy and devotion which ought to feed the fear of God. A politician who is moved by fear of man, and who tacks and trims to avoid his hostility, can never retain an efficient thought of God. So it is with a minister who is afraid of man; his mind is not filled with a vision of "the Lord high and lifted up." But, indeed, the same is true of anybody. If the barometer we consult for our guidance is the opinion and conventions of man, God Himself will be nothing. If we are always consulting man, moved and governed by his expediencies, God will vanish away. "The fear of man is a snare," and the power of the snare is found in its fascination to allure our minds from the Lord of Hosts. "Afraid of a man that shall die, and forget-test the Lord thy Maker."

And here is another type from the portrait gallery of the Bible. "Thou hast forgotten the God of thy salvation, and hast not been mindful of the Rock of thy strength." Here is a forgetfulness that is born when we have recovered from some weakness. Pride of strength makes us forget the rock out of which we were hewn. This is a most common and insidious peril. Our weakness helps our remembrance of God; our strength is the friend of forgetfulness. Perhaps this is most apparent in our physical weakness. In our weakness we remember the Lord, and the dim things of the unseen come clearly into view. But when our strength is regained the vivid vision fades again, and is sometimes entirely lost. And so our strength is really our drug. It is an opiate which ministers to spiritual forgetfulness. And so it is with every kind of strength. Frailty in any direction makes us lean upon the power of the Almighty, and in every frailty our remembrance of Him is keen and clear. But our strength helps to create a feeling of independence, and we become unmindful of our God. And therefore it is that a man who never knows weakness has a stupendous task in maintaining communion with God. People who never know what it is to be ill have so many more barriers to overcome in their fellowship with the Unseen.

And here is a third Scriptural type of spiritual forgetfulness. "They have gone from mountain to hill, and have forgotten their resting-places." It is the figure of a flock of wandering sheep roaming away over the distant hills and mountains. They have gone from one place to another, and in the range of their goings have forgotten their place of rest. Their very vagrancy has made them insensible to their real home. That is to say, their vagrancy has induced forgetfulness.

Now I think this word is very descriptive of much of our modern life. It is a vagrancy rather than a crusade. We go from "mountain to hill," and from hill to mountain. We are always on the move. We are for ever seeking something else and never finding satisfaction. We get weary and tired with one thing and we trudge to another! We are here, there, and yonder, and our lives become jaded and stale. But the extraordinary thing is that in all our goings we forget our resting-place. "Return unto thy rest, O my soul." Yes, but we turn anywhere and everywhere rather than to this. Our lives can become so vagrant that God is exiled from our minds. It seems as though there is something in vagrancy that stupefies the soul, and renders us insensitive to our true home and rest in God.

When I first came to New York, during the first few months of my ministry, .I was continually asked by people, "Have you got into the whirl?" The very phrase seems so far removed from the words of the psalmist, "He maketh me to lie down in green pastures. He leadeth me beside the still waters." Not that the psalmist luxuriated in indolence, or spent his days in the fatness of ease; the rest was only preparative to a march. "He leadeth me in the paths of righteousness." But from the march he returned to his resting-place. But we can be caught in such a whirl in our modern life that we just rush from one thing to another, and we forget the glorious rest that is ours in God. I think the enemy of our souls must love to get us into a whirl! If once we are dizzied with sensations we are likely to lose the thought of God. "They have gone from the mountain to the hill, and have forgotten their resting-place."

Let me give one further example from the Word of God. "According to their pasture, so were they filled; they were filled, and their heart was exalted; therefore have they forgotten Me." Here is a rich pasturage, and in the enjoyment of it there is born the spirit of forgetfulness. And surely this is

22

the stupefaction of abundance. In Southern France, where attar of roses is distilled, a very curious ailment imperils the workers. The very abundance of the rose-leaves induces a sort of sleeping-sickness. And surely it is even so in the abundances that are sometimes given to man. They are prone to sink him into the sleep of spiritual forgetfulness.

A man's devotion is apt to dwindle as he becomes more successful. Our piety does not keep pace with our purse. Absorption in bounty makes us forgetful of the Giver. We can be so concerned in the pasturage that the Shepherd is forgotten. Our very fulness is apt to become our foe. Our clearest visions are given us in the winter-time when nature is scanty and poor. The fulness of the leaf blocks the outlook and the distance is hid. And the summer-time of life, when leaves and flowers are plentiful, is apt to bring a veil. And the very plentifulness impedes our communion.

These are some of the types of forgetfulness which are mentioned and described in the Word of God. Is there any help for us? There is a very gracious promise of the Master in which I think all these perils are anticipated, and in the strength of which they can be met and overcome: "He shall teach you all things, and bring all things to your remembrance, whatsoever I have said unto you." Here is the promise of a gracious minister to the memory, strengthening it in its hold upon the unseen. I suppose that one of the most urgent needs of the common life is the sanctification of the memory. If the memory were to be really hallowed it would forget many things which it now remembers, and it would certainly remember many things which it now forgets. We are apt to retain worthless things, and destructive things, things that ought to have been dropped and buried and left in their graves in past years. But we carry them with us to our undoing. The ministry of the Holy Spirit will deal with this unwise retention, and will make a memory leaky where it is wise for it to lose. But, more than that, it will strengthen its powers of spiritual comprehension, and will enable it to keep hold of the unseen and the eternal. What should I most like to remember? I should like to remember with unfailing constancy the glorious, holy Being of the eternal God. I should like to remember the unspeakable ministry of His grace, which worked in my redemption in Christ Jesus, my Lord. I should like to remember the benefits of His daily providence which shine along my road in unfailing succession. I should like to remember the eternal significance of transient events, and hold the lessons of yesterday's happenings to guide me in my march to-day. And when new occasions and new duties arise, and I am face to face with novel circumstances, I should like to be reminded of those words of the Lord Jesus which would give me the needful illumination: "He shall bring all things to your remembrance, whatsoever I have said unto you."

IV. SPIRITUAL ABILITIES

THE apostolic life abounds in suggestions of power. It is not only that there is power in some particular direction, there is basal executive force which gives impetus to everything. The life is filled with "go" and "drive" and strength of character and conduct. Power resides behind every faculty, and every disposition, and every form of service. The life is efficient and effective. It is as though a man had a fine equipment of tools, but his hand is weak and trembling, and suddenly there is given to him a mighty strength of grip, and he is able to seize upon every tool and make it accomplish its appointed purpose. "Ye shall receive power when the Holy Ghost is come upon you," and that energy empowered everything, and gave intensity and strength in every exercise of the apostle's life. Let us look at one or two directions in which this holy power was revealed.

The apostolic life was distinguished by the strength of its relationship to God. It was powerful in its ability to believe. We can do nothing more vital to any man than to encourage and strengthen his finest faith. When our faith in the Highest is limp and uncertain everything lacks assurance. When there is lameness in the movements of the spirit our conduct can never be firm. And therefore did the Holy Spirit energize the early apostles in their supreme relationships, and steadied them in their faith. Now, faith is first of all an attitude and then an act. It is primarily a spiritual posture which reveals itself in moral obedience. And to be rich in faith is to possess a poise of soul which steadily contemplates and rests in the love of God, in sunshine and in shower, and through all the changing seasons and temperatures of our years. When the soul is thus quietly steadied in this spiritual assurance, its faith is expressed in manifold holy . ministries of hope and love. This ability of faith is one of the radiant characteristics of the early Church, and it was the creation of the Holy Ghost.

But just as apostolic life was empowered in its relationship to God, so was it quietly empowered in its resistances to the enemy of God. There are two phrases used by the Apostle Paul, in which this sovereign ability is described, "able to resist the wiles," "able to quench the darts." I do not know any third way in which the enemy of God approaches the souls of men. He draws near to us in wiles, he dresses himself in all kinds of flattering guises, he exercises himself in deceitful mimicries, he uses glosses innumerable. He disguises the ugly by throwing about it a seductive limelight. He hides his destructiveness in bowers of roses. The Boers used to send their ammunition about in piano cases; and this is a fitting symbol of many of the stratagems of our foe. He comes to us as an angel of light, hiding the lightning which is his peculiar equipment. He makes the broad way fascinating, while the narrow way often appears repellent. The entrance to the broad way is marked by a glittering crown, while a heavy cross is hidden not far away. The entrance to the narrow way is marked by a cross, but the crown of life is not far away.

And so, all through the generations, this wily antagonist has been seeking to ensnare the children of God. He uses attractive euphemisms. He deceives us by grand speech. He makes us think we are striding out in glorious liberty when we are really moving in servitude. Now, one of the great distinctions of apostolic life was the power to discern and resist the insidiousness of the foe. Their eyes were anointed with grace, and they were able to pierce the mere appearance of things and to discriminate between the holy and the profane. They could distinguish mere ease from holy peace, and all transient flimsiness from the things that abide. And this vigilance and strength were the equipment of the Holy Ghost. He kept the soul awake and vigorous, and they were not taken by surprise.

But another apostolic ability is expressed in the kindred phrase, "able to quench the darts of the evil one." For sometimes the enemy comes to us in sudden flame, and not in seductive light. He leaps upon us in an irritation rather than steals upon us in some soothing consolation. Some inflammatory suggestion is flung across the threshold of the mind, and our life is all ablaze. The fiery dart finds congenial material and life is consumed with unholy passion. A spark from a passing engine can kindle a fire which can destroy a countryside; and the spark of an infernal suggestion, or the merest hint of criticism, or some transient incident can convert the soul of the unwary into a house of unclean fire. Now, these early apostles had a power to quench these darts. It is a wonderful equipment to be kept so cool and quiet in disposition that when the inflammatory thing is thrown it finds nothing congenial and speedily dies out. This is the ministry of the Comforter.

Breathe through the pulses of desire

Thy coolness and thy balm.

And this "cooling" is the blessed service which the Holy One fulfils in the souls who entertain Him as their guest.

But there is still a third kind of power distinguished in apostolic life in relation to the evil one. It is "mighty to the pulling down of strongholds." Every generation is face to face with established devilry. Castellated wrong rears itself on every side. There are great vested interests built upon iniquity. Vice lifts itself in very proud mien. Wickedness builds itself a lofty palace. Injustice girds itself with legality. Mischief is formed by a law. There are strongholds of iniquity. Every great reformer has levelled his attack upon a stronghold. There were many in the days of the early Church, and a great many still remain; and our power of assault, definite in aim and invincible in attack, is to be found in the indwelling and fellowship of that mighty Advocate who is Himself also the Minister of our peace.

There is a third great relationship in which the New Testament describes the power of those who are in communion with the Holy. Ghost, and that is their power in their relationship to the children of men. "With great power gave the apostles witness." That is an ability which distinguished the early Church, the power to arrest the indifferent by the proclamation of spiritual truth, and by the confession of spiritual experience. Their words were weighted with the significance which crashed through opposition. How empty our words can be! The Turks have been deceived into using empty cartridges, and the ministers of the kingdom are often victims of a like deception. We indulge in empty words, and the men on the strongholds laugh at our impotence. There is nothing more tragical than the employment of forceless speech. But when there is life in the word, how tremendous is its passage! "The words that I speak unto you, they are spirit and they are life." They do not drop like dead lead, or like dead feathers; they go forth like living ministers endowed with the terrific life of God. The Holy Spirit is the indwelling Partner who fills our cartridges, who endows our speech, and makes our words the very vehicles of heavenly power and grace.

Wing my words that they may reach

The hidden depths of many a heart.

There is one other power which I should like to name, which is mentioned in the apostolic record: "Able to comfort." Is there any gift more gracious than this--to have a wallet filled with oil and wine, that when we meet the bruised and the fainting we can minister healing and inspiration? Is there any more beautiful ministry to which any child of man can be called? To be able to speak words that console, to have a presence that heartens and cheers, to give a witness that lifts the despondent into the light of hope; this may be the privilege of all the friends of Christ Jesus. They may have a ministry in time of sorrow like that of sunlight falling upon dark clouds. They may go down the gloomy ways of men, lighting lamps of encouragement and hope. "Able to comfort!" They have the power to apprehend the ailment and the sorrow, and they have the equipment to soothe and to bless. "Ye shall receive such power when the Holy Ghost is come upon you."

I feel that all this is only as a little handful of the abilities mentioned in the Word of God as distinguishing those who are the companions of the Holy Ghost. I return to the word with which I began. Spiritual power, as given to us by God, is executive power, lying behind all our faculties and dispositions. It is a fundamental dynamic, and in it everything finds its strength. Here, therefore, we must place the emphasis in our quest of a stronger life. We must seek the communion of the Holy Ghost. This is the originating fellowship in which vision is born, and ideals are realized, and in which the soul is adorned with the grace of our Lord and Saviour Jesus Christ.

V. CHRIST'S HABIT OF PRAYER

I WANT to consider Christ's habit of private prayer. In the first place, it is very significant that He prayed at all. Jesus of Nazareth had every form of strength which men associate with masculine life. He had strength of body. He had strength of mind. He had strength of purpose and will. He had marvellous strength of affection. He had strength to move amid foul conditions without catching their contagion. He had extraordinary strength of patience. He was absolutely fearless in the presence of hostility. He was calm and undaunted when assailed by official religion. He had every form of strength which men count admirable. And this man prayed. He was constantly praying, and He was the strongest who ever trod the ways of men. I want to consider two or three occasions in His earthly life when we find Him at prayer.

First of all, then, I find Him in prayer when temptation drew near. I am not now thinking of that early experience in His life which is known to us as the Temptation. I turn from that desert experience to another which came to Him in the thick of His ministry, after the purpose of His redemptive ministry had been revealed. I choose the hour which preceded the Transfiguration. Nothing is said about the tempter; but unless I utterly misread the incident, and misinterpret the secrets of common life, the temptation was fierce and acute. The Lord had manifested His love. He had declared His gracious purpose. He had sealed His testimony with His deeds. Already He was shedding His blood in sacrificial service. And with what results? The horizon was blackening with omens of rejection. The storm of hostility was brewing. The air was thick with suspicion, derision, and contempt. Unfriendly eyes glared upon Him from every side. "He came unto His own, and His own received Him not." And just then, when the elements were gathering for tempests, I read these words: "He went up into a mountain to pray." And why did He go? Before Him there stretched the darkening road to appalling desolation. Yonder loomed the cross. And this was the temptation which, I think, approached His soul: "Is it worth while?" Should He go on to night and crucifixion, or there and then finish with translation? Reverently I believe these were the alternatives in those days of gathering gloom. Should He choose an immediate re-entry into "the glory which I had with Thee before the world was," or a re-entry into the world of resentment where dwelt the evil spirits of malice and rejection? Should He finish there or go on to the bitter end? "He prayed," and while He prayed He made His choice. He would go down to the scene of rejection, down to the waiting multitude, down to the envious eyes, down to the malicious designs, down to the cross.

"And as He prayed the fashion of His countenance was altered." And no wonder! We are always transfigured when we make choice of the Divine will. There came a voice to Him saying, "This is My beloved Son." "And they came down from the mountain, and much people met Him."

Have we not known a similar hour, as far as our own limitations would permit? Have we never been tempted to ask i f a certain bit of blood-demanding work was worth while? Have we not had pointed out to us the flippancy of those we tried to help, their indifference, their levity, their contempt, and have we not felt the enticement to lay the task down? There is that bit of work we have tried to do on the City Council. We have laboured for years. We have been exposed to the insults of contested elections. And there is our quiet home, with the wife and children, and the slippers and the books. Shall we choose the abode of comfort, or return again to difficult service? Shall we put on our slippers or stride out again on the heavy, thorny road? Just at seasons like these and at that juncture Jesus prayed, and while He was on His knees He made His choice.

Let us look at the Master again in the habit of prayer. "And He healed many that were sick of divers diseases, and cast out many devils . . . and He departed into a solitary place and there prayed." But what need was there to pray just then? He was most evidently engaged in doing good. The newly-opened eyes of the blind were radiant with thanksgiving. The once lame man leaped as a hart. The Master abounded in good works, and some measure of popular favour rested upon Him. Then why go apart to pray?

First of all, He retired to pray in order to provide against nervous exhaustion. All this healing, all this giving, all this sympathy meant large expenditure of vital power. "Virtue is gone out of Me." And, therefore, He prayed in order that His vital resources might be restored. There is some work that cannot be done without resort to Divine communion. When the soul is drained in the ministry of sympathy, there is nothing for it but resort to the springs, and there is nothing which so readily and powerfully restores a man like drinking the water of life. "They that wait upon the Lord shall renew their strength."

But there is a second reason why our Saviour prayed when He was in the midst of successful public work. He prayed in order to make His soul secure against the perils of success, against "the destruction that wasteth at noonday." Success may bruise the spirit more than failure. Heat can ruin a violin quite as effectually as the chilly damp. Prosperity slays many a man whose health was preserved in adversity. Robert Burns was never the same after the glamour of Edinburgh. And so I think our Lord prayed in the hour of popular favour lest His very success should maim His life of service. And there is significant counsel in His practice for all the children of men. When we are busily successful, let us pray, and we need not "be afraid for the arrow that flieth by day."

There is one other occasion in our Master's life of prayer to which I want to lead the thoughts of my readers. "Now it came to pass in those days that He went out into a mountain to pray, and continued all night in prayer to God. And when it was day He called unto Him His disciples, and of them He chose twelve." There was a night of prayer, and then there was a great decision. Our Lord took time to pray before He made a momentous choice.

We in our own degree have similar choices to make, both in our individual and corporate life. We have to choose our careers. We have to make choice of turnings in the ever-winding way. We have to choose our representatives in the City Council and in Parliament. We have to choose ministers and deacons, and in a hundred other ways serious decisions have to be made. Why should we pray? We must, first of all, pray in order that big considerations might possess the mind. We are prone to live amid small motives, tiny purposes, belittling prejudices, partial and lop-sided ambitions. And there is nothing kills little things like our prayers. If we take our politics into the realm of prayer, it is impossible for us to remain wretched partisans. We may give a party vote, but our vision will reach beyond the bounds of party, and through a party triumph we shall seek the extension of the kingdom of God. When we pray we move into the realm of big things, big motives, big sympathies, big ideals. The biggest outlooks come to us when we are on our knees. And so, when we are making big decisions, let us find time to pray, in order that the matters may be greatly decided, and that all little and belittling intrusions may be effectually destroyed.

And so, if we are truly wise, we shall surely pray. To cease to pray is to build up the windows of the soul, to close the ventilators, to shut out air and light, to immure the soul in an atmosphere devoid of inspiration. And yet it is possible so to pray that the spirit of prayer shall determine all our purposes, and all our purposes shall be fit to steal into our prayers. A friend said of Dr. Westcott that "he read and worked in the very mind in which he prayed, and his prayer was of singular intensity." That is a great and gracious attainment, and I think we can all share the wonderful triumph which mingles prayerful aspiration with common toil.

VI. THE THANKFULNESS OF JESUS

I WANT to lead the meditation of my readers to one of the private habits of our Lord--His habit of thanksgiving. Everyone who knows the New Testament knows how the apostolic life abounded in praise. It runs like some singing river through all their .changing days. And where did they learn the habit? They had got it from their Lord. The Master's habit must have made a profound impression upon them. There must have been something very distinct and distinctive about it. We are told that the two disciples, journeying to Emmaus after the awful happenings in Jerusalem, recognized their risen Lord when He began to give thanks. "He was made known to them in the breaking of bread." They knew Him by His gratitude and by the manner in which He expressed it. He was recognized by His praise. Let us recall two or three examples of this shining habit of our Lord.

"And Jesus took the loaves and gave thanks." That is to say, He took commonplace, common bread, and associated it with God, and it was no longer a commonplace. He gave thanks, and in the recognition the common was revealed as the Divine. The ordinary meal became a sacrament with the Unseen Presence as real as we apprehend Him at the table of the Lord.

Now, a man who feels the divine relationships of bread will have a very transfigured road. The man whose praise is elicited by loaves will also be thankful for the cornfield, the sunshine, the dew, and the rain, for the reapers who gather the corn, for the touch of God in the labourer, and for the millstones which grind the corn that makes the bread. He who took the loaves and gave thanks would also give thanks for the common lily of the field, the daisy of His native land. Indeed, I think we may truly say that the Master's habit of praise made every common thing radiant, and every wayside bush became aflame with God. He breathed His music of gratitude through the commonest reeds.

Now unless His disciples can do the same, unless we can touch and feel God in the commonplaces, He is going to be a very infrequent and unfamiliar Guest. For life is made up of very ordinary experiences. Now and again a novelty leaps into the way, but the customary tenor is rarely broken. It is the ordinary stars that shine upon us night after night; it is only occasionally that a comet comes our way. Look at some of the daily commonplaces--health, sleep, bread and butter, work, friendship, a few flowers by the wayside, the laughter of children, the ministry of song, the bright day, the cool night--if I do not perceive God in these things I have a very unhallowed and insignificant road. On the other hand, the man who discovers the Divine in a loaf of bread, and lifts his song of praise, has a wonderful world, for divinity will call to him on every side.

I do not know how we can better begin to cultivate the Master's habit than by beginning with daily bread. Because if we begin with bread we cannot possibly end there. If we see one commonplace lit up with God, other commonplaces will begin to be illumined, until life will be like some city seen from a height by night, with all the common lamps in the common streets burning and shining with mystic flame. So let us begin with bread. But let us give thanks reverently, not with the sudden tap and the sharp, superficial sentence of a public dinner. Let us do it quietly, apprehendingly, with an effort to realize the presence of the awful, gracious, merciful God. And let us do it without formality, and seeking deliverance from the perilous opiate of words. Let us change our phraseology, let us sometimes bow in silence, and share the significant, worshipful stillness of the Friends.

Let us watch our Master again and listen to His praise. "I thank Thee, Father, Lord of heaven and earth, that Thou hast hid these things from the wise and prudent, and hast revealed them unto babes." Our Master thanks the Father that spiritual secrets are not the perquisites of culture, that it is not by cleverness that we gain access into the Kingdom of Grace. He gives thanks that "these things" have not been made dependent upon academic knowledge, that they are not the prizes of the merely clever and acute, but that they are "revealed unto babes."

Now, mark this: Out of six men only one may be clever, only one may have the advantage of knowledge, but all six may have the elementary simplicities of a child. All cannot be "knowing," but all can be docile. All cannot be "cute," but all can be humble. All cannot be "learned," but all can be trustful. All cannot attain to mental sovereignty, but all may sit on thrones of sovereign love. And it is upon what all may have that our Lord fixes His eye; it is the common denominator for which He offers His praise. He takes bread, the commonplace of life, and gives thanks; He takes the child, the commonalty among men, and gives thanks. He offers praise for the commonplaces and the commonalties. He gives thanks for the things that are common to Erasmus and Billy Bray, to Spurgeon and John Jaspar, to Onesimus and St. Paul. To give thanks for commonplaces makes a transfigured world; to give thanks for commonalties makes a transfigured race. The one unveils the world as our Father's house; the other unveils the race as our Father's family.

Now, would it not be good to exercise ourselves in that form of praise? Would it not be wise to allow our minds to rove over the race of men irrespective of class and condition, and search out the commonalties and sing our song of praise? One thing such praise would do for us. It would preserve in our minds a vivid sense of the relative values of things. We should recognize that academic learning is not to be mentioned in comparison with loneliness, that carnal power has not the holy standing of meekness, and that mere eminence is not to be counted in the same world with love. What we may have in common with the poorest and most ignorant is our most precious possession.

Look at the Master once more. "Then they took away the stone from the place where the dead was laid. And Jesus lifted up His eyes and said, Father, I thank Thee that Thou hast heard Me." The Master gave thanks before the miracle was wrought, while the dead was still lying stiff and stark in the tomb. He offered praise not for the victory attained but for victory about to be won. His song was not for what He had received, but for what He was about to receive. He gave thanks before the dead marched forth, and before the mourners' tears were dried. The doxology was sung at the beginning and not at the end.

"Father, I thank Thee . . ." "And when He had thus spoken He cried with a loud voice, Lazarus, come forth, and he that was dead came forth." The sound of praise thrilled through the call that awaked the dead.

Have we learned the habit? Is that the gracious order of our thought and labour? Sometimes we thank God for food we are about to receive. Do we thank God for power we are about to receive? Do we thank God for victory we are about to receive? Do I go forth in the morning to the warfare of the day with thanks for coming victory filling me with exhilaration and powerful hope? Did I rear my altar of praise before I took my sword? Is that how I go to the pulpit, thanking God for victories about to be won? Is that how I go to my class, quietly confident in the coming of my Lord? Is that how I take up the work of social reform? Is the song of victory in the air before I enter the field? Can I begin to sing the song of harvest home as I go forth to sow the seed? Am I sure of God, so sure that I can sing as soon as the struggle begins? That was the Master's way. It was first the thanks and then the miracle.

And so Jesus assumed that His prayer was answered before He addressed the dead. And the significance of the act is this. To gratefully assume that prayers for power are answered opens the entire being to the full and gracious influence of the answer. Gratitude opens the channels of the whole life to the incoming of the Divine. There is no mood so receptive as praise; it fills the soul with the fulness of God, and the indwelling God works wonders, even to the raising of the dead.

I have given these three examples of the Master's habit of thanksgiving. It is our great wisdom to follow in His train. All manner of things are promised to the grateful heart. Thanksgiving is to be a minister of vigilant sight; "watch in the same with thanksgiving." Thanksgiving is to be a stimulant to a jaded and weary soul: "Be not drunken with wine, . . . but be ye thankful." Thanksgiving is to be a beautifier of the regenerate soul. Ten lepers were purified, only one was beautified; "he returned to give thanks." And, lastly, thanksgiving glorifies God. It is by the brightness of our praise that we offer the best witness to the goodness and power of our God.

VII. THE MAGIC TOUCH

WHO does not remember the fascinating fairy who filled our childhood with wonders, and whose magic wand used to change worn-out shoes into silver slippers, and tattered, ragged garments into princely attire, and dust-heaps into gardens full of bright and perfumed flowers? How we followed the gracious fairy in her transforming ways!

But fairyland is gone, and fairy wonder is dead. Our years have passed, and life has become sombre with care, dashed with sorrow, grey with disappointment, and withered and blighted by sin and shame. If only something analogous to the romance of childhood could steal back into the sombre years of manhood! If only out of the unseen spaces some mystic spirit would appear who could transform dulled and blighted character, and transform dulled and blighted circumstances, how busy he would be! Well, here is an announcement of His coming, and this is what He claims to do! "To give unto them beauty for ashes, the oil of joy for mourning, and the garment of praise for the spirit of heaviness." It sounds like the evangel of some gracious magician. It will be well worth while to consider His ways.

"Beauty for ashes," and the beauty here suggested is the coronet or diadem of a bride. Some humiliated, sinful soul, soiled with self-abuse, worn and torn, wearied and ashamed, is flinging the ashes of her penitence toward heaven, and letting them fall upon her head. Those ashes are the emblems of a burnt-out and wasted day, and she is flinging them towards the heavens in open confession of her shame, if, perchance, the dead embers might be made to glow again. And what does the gentle Lord offer this depressed and tainted soul? He offers her the coronet of a bride. He will make the dejected exile the wife of the Lamb. The poor, wearied drudge of sin is to be honoured by becoming the consort of the Holy God.

What, then, is there in the figure? There is the wonderful love and devotion of the eternal, loving God. God loves the most wretched, dejected, sin-blasted soul on earth, and lie would encircle that soul with the diadem of the bride! If that be true, the love of God is the biggest thing we can think about, and the most wonderful theme in human speech. If we only realize that love on the authority of His Word, life will be illumined and glorified with a far more wonderful light than that which fills the soul of a young girl when first she hears the whispered word that tells the story of a pure and manly love.

"Oil of joy for mourning," and this is coronation oil, consecration oil, the oil significant of the endowment of regal authority and power. Who are to receive coronation? Those whose souls are filled with mourning. The mourning is the cry of defeat. It is the wail of the failure. It is the moan of the broken. It is the pathetic cry of the disordered, the men and women who have fallen, who have succumbed in moral and spiritual calamity. That is to say, the good Lord offers the crown of restored sovereignty to the children of moral disorder. He offers restored regality to those who have "gone to pieces." He offers coronation to those who have lost their crowns, sovereignty for those who are bruised and broken. "He raiseth up the poor out of the dust, and lifteth the needy out of the dunghill, that He may set him with princes." He will transform the slave into a monarch. "He crowneth thee with loving-kindness and tender mercies."

"The garment of praise for the spirit of heaviness," and the heaviness is that of dimness and failing light, light trembling on the verge of eclipse. There are people whose lives are like that. There is no heat about them, and no radiance. They are cold, dull, cheerless, funereal, shut in by encompassing gloom. And the Magician comes, and He offers to change that gloomy, sombre attire for the garment of praise. For heaviness He will give buoyancy, the joy of the bridal feast for heavy-footed woe.

Surely this, bright, regal, bridal attire is what is lacking in the religious life of to-day. There is something wrong with our nobility when it is not crowned with radiance. There is something wrong with our goodwill when it does not bear the hall-mark of good cheer. There is something wrong with our communion when we are not "children of light." When the bridal attire is missing there is little or nothing about us to suggest that we are the brides of the Lamb. How are men and women to know that we are of the King's household if we do not wear "the garments of salvation"? How can they believe that we have gazed upon the Divine glory if we do not wear the splendours of "the garment of praise"?

I remember two significant sentences in one of Robert Louis Stevenson's letters, which express the common judgment of the world: "I do not call that by the name of religion which fills a man with bile. If a man is surly, filled with a dull and bitter disposition, if he be sombre and melancholy, how can he witness to the glories of the eternal life?" And the other sentence is this: "I will think more of his prayers when I see in him a spirit of praise." Stevenson wanted to see common gratitude before he received the witness of a clamant piety. If our religion does not clothe us in the refinements of common courtesies it will fail to win the interested attention of the men of the world. A fine spiritual grace, nobly worn, is a great witness for the Lord. The distinction between the Church and the world ought to be found in the difference of their habits. The elect ought to prove their relationship by the beauty of their moral and spiritual attire.

Do we believe that the transformation is possible? Have we full confidence in the power of the Great Magician? Do we believe that He will exchange a coronet for ashes, joyous sovereignty for sullen despair, and a garment of radiant cheerfulness for the spirit of gloom? If we do not believe it, where is our gospel? If we do not believe it, where is our life? The Almighty God can transform the most ungracious and unwelcome life. When He touches barrenness, "the wilderness and the solitary place become glad, and the desert rejoices and blossoms like the rose." And so we can in this great faith confront all the deformities of our time. Only in the Lord Jesus can these deformities be made straight. When legislation has done its utmost, when education has had its last word, the waste place will still remain, and only by the immediate personal Presence of the Great Magician can it be made beautiful as the paradise of God.

VIII. THE BEQUEST OF PEACE

"MY peace I give unto you." These words gain immensely deepened significance from the circumstances in which they were spoken. When we put them into their surroundings they shine like a radiant gem with a foil of dark background. When the Lord spake these words He was not resting in the domestic love and quietness of the home at Bethany. The air was thick with rumours, and the betrayer had gone out, and was even now engaged in his treacherous mission. Even Peter's loyalty threatened to surrender to evil popular will. Crucifixion was not twenty-four hours away. Christ's enemies were at the very gate. It was in circumstances like these, turbulent and stormy, that our Lord quietly claimed to be in possession of deep and mysterious peace.

"Peace I leave with you." The form of the speech is that of a customary salutation or farewell. "Whatsoever house ye enter let your peace be upon it." But our Lord's speech is widely different from the common convention. People had fallen into the habit of saying "Peace" as we have got into the habit of saying "Good-morning" or "Goodbye," and there was as little vital content in one as in the other. The salutation had lost its sanctity. It had become a formality of life. The customary speech was used just to break an awkward silence; the Lord's was used to renew and enrich the heart. The conventional speech was idly ceremonial; the Lord's was a gracious achievement. At the best, the popular speech was an expression of affability; the Lord's benediction was an invaluable bequest. When He said "Peace," there was something accomplished, something done. It was not an affair of empty words; it was a glorious transaction. "The words that I speak unto you, they are spirit, they are life." The salutation was, therefore, vital and effective; it was a holy minister, conveying inconceivable treasures to the hearts of men.

"My peace I give unto you." What is the nature of this peace? First of all it is rightness with God. When the Lord Jesus Christ brings His own peace into the hearts of men, they become inherently sound by becoming fundamentally at one with God. It is very significant that the radical meaning of the original word is suggestive of union; two sundered things are brought together again. And the gift of peace means a recovery of healthy fellowship between the soul .and the eternal God. Now let it be understood at once that the gift of peace does not imply perfection. There may be a general "rightness" in the relationship between man and wife, and yet there may be an occasional misunderstanding, even a temporary outburst of temper, while nothing fundamental becomes crooked or perverse. A general "rightness" or healthiness of the body is consistent with an occasional chill or superficial scratch or pain. There may be a temporary derangement while the heart is as sound as a bell. Our Lord acknowledged this possibility in His own gracious teachings. Men may be essentially right with God who are not yet by any means perfect. Even a man who has been bathed "needeth to wash his feet." And so peace consists essentially in this innermost "rightness" with God. The general life tends toward the highest. Its primary ambitions are fixed upon the good pleasure of God. There is intimacy of fellowship. There is an open road. There is a ladder of communion, on which the angels ascend and descend continually. The peace that the Lord gives enables the soul to say with glad humility, "I and my Father are one."

And secondly, if peace is fundamental rightness with God, it is also fundamental union with God's universe. Natural forces become the friendly allies of men who are right with God. "The whole creation groaneth and waiteth for the manifestation of the children of God." When a man is one with the Maker he has the co-operation of all the Maker has made. The winds and currents are his friends. "The stars in their courses" fight on his side. There is established "a covenant between him and the stones of the field." And so peace is the condition of the soul in its God-purposed relationship of being right with Him and one with the movements of the Divine order in the world.

Now, our Lord had this peace. It was His through all His changing days. It was independent of seasons, and He had it "in the dark and cloudy day." And, therefore, there are certain things we can say about it. This peace can exist in the midst of apparent defeat. It does not require success to assure one of its presence. We can have God's peace and yet be apparent failures in the world. For look at our Saviour Himself. Look at His position when the words were uttered. The antagonism of the multitude was approaching culmination. Despite His wealth of gracious deeds He was everywhere met with deep and fierce resentment. Even His own disciples pathetically misunderstood His mission. After a training of three years, when He had daily led them into the realm of the Spirit and into communion with the Highest, they had just been quarrelling one with another, "Who should be greatest." One of the disciples was the victim of greed, and he deliberately sold his Lord for thirty pieces of silver. The rest of the disciples were becoming fearful, and the mood of desertion was upon them. Crucifixion was at hand. What an apparent failure! From the worldly point of view everything had gone wrong. And yet, in spite of everything, the Lord retained His condition of peace. And so it may be with the Lord's disciples. The applause of men may not gratify our ears. No worldly garland may be put upon our brow. We may climb unto no high place in the world's esteem. We may stumble along a painful way, we may be continually jostled and elbowed into the rear of the competing crowd, and yet we may have fundamental "rightness" with God and share with Jesus the condition of heavenly peace.

If Jesus Christ had this peace, then its possession does not make us incapable of sorrow. No; it would be more true to say that this peace makes us more capable of sorrow, for to be right with God is to be sensitive to His joys and sorrows, and to share them. The Master who spake about "My peace" wept over Jerusalem, and His heart was torn by the contemplation of the sins of the city. He wept by the grave of Lazarus as He called to mind the accumulated common sorrows of the world. He wept over the vagrant, aimless multitude, for what is "compassion" but a most refined and delicate form of grief? He saw that the crowd was wayward and vagrant, purposeless, moving here and there in constant danger, and He pitied the crowd with a pity that redeemed it. Thus the Lord had an infinite capacity for sorrow, and yet He was in possession of peace. It is even so with His disciples. The Apostle Paul used words which are seemingly inconsistent with one another, "What sorrow I have!" "What travail!" "How I agonize!" And yet he could also speak of "The peace of God which passeth understanding." He was fundamentally right with God, but the fountain of tears was not dried up.

Peace, perfect peace, with sorrows surging round?

On Jesus' bosom naught but peace is found.

And then, in the third place, it is evident that the possession of peace does not banish the possibility of temptation. Our Master, who claimed the possession of peace, was tempted on every side. He had the temptations that besiege the flesh and seek the unlawful gratification of appetite. He had the temptations which assail the mind and seek to entice it to mental presumption. He had the temptations which waylay the soul and seek to seduce it into illicit homage. And these temptations were repeated throughout His life. He was essentially at one with the Father, and yet temptations were never away from His door. It is well for us to remember this. We are sometimes inclined to suspect the reality of our union with God by the number and prevalence of our snares. We are apt to regard our temptations as signs of our detachment from the Master. We may be at peace when temptations crowd the field. "Thou preparest a table before me in the presence of mine enemies." God's saints have in all generations sat at that table, and their souls have been filled with holy laughter in the confidence of their God.

Now this wonderful peace is the gift of the Lord Jesus. "I give unto you." All that is requisite for us to possess the gift is in the power of the Lord Jesus.

In Him we have the forgiveness of sin. In Him we obtain the mystic union with our God. In Him we find the secret strength of holy continuance. All are "His and His alone." This peace is not the perquisite of some particular temperament. It is not the attainment of painful effort and service. It is not the refined fruit of prolonged culture. It is a legacy. "Peace I leave with you." It is a gift; "My peace I give unto you." "He is our peace."

And there are two ways in which this gift of peace differs from the gifts of the world. In the first place, it differs in the matter of the gift. When the world seeks to give peace it addresses itself to conditions; the Lord addresses Himself to character. The world deals with things; the Lord deals with kinships. The world keeps in the material realm; Jesus Christ moves in the spiritual realm. The world offers to put us into a fine house; the Lord offers to make a fine tenant. The world will introduce us into "fine society"; Jesus will make us at home with God.

In the second place, our Lord differs from the world in the manner of His giving. The world always gives its best at the beginning. It offers gaudy garlands, brimming cups, and glittering crowns. "But knowest thou not it shall be bitterness in the latter end?" It makes an imposing fire, but we are speedily left with the ashes. It leads us to a showy feast, but we soon encounter aches and pains. It blinds us with the "garish day"; then come chill twilight and uncompanionable night. "Not as the world giveth give I." He keeps His good wine until last. He leads us from grace to grace, from faith to faith, from glory to glory. "Greater things than these shall we see." His gifts grow deeper, richer, fuller, right through the eternal years.

IX. SEEKING THE BEST

"THE Kingdom of Heaven is like unto a merchantman seeking goodly pearls." This sentence gives us one great characteristic of the kingly life, for the inhabitants of the Kingdom of Heaven are the kingly men and women. They move in great stateliness through the Word of God. They are distinguished by humility and dignity, by a certain retirement which is allied with the most mysterious glory. Great images are used to suggest the greatness of their character. They move in impressive lordship and liberty. They are kings and priests unto God. And here I say is one of their distinctions; they are seeking goodly pearls.

And so the kingly life is a life in quest of big things. Everyone is painfully familiar with the temptation to fritter away life in interests that are small and mean. There are many Scriptural types of the wasteful and belittled life. There are those who spend their strength in seeking money. The concentrated purpose of their days is a quest for gold. They are zealous for artificial gems and they miss the goodly pearls. Judas Iscariot had the priceless privilege of communion with his Lord. He had the incomparable glory of living with the Master day by day--the opportunity of entering into the "inheritance of the saints in light," and he used his privilege in the quest for money, and all that he got out of his supreme advantage was thirty pieces of silver. He missed the pearls.

And here is another Scriptural type described as "lovers of pleasure more than lovers of God." They sought the transitory rather than the eternal. They were more intent upon the carnal than the Divine. They were out seeking rockets and ignoring dawns. All that they got from life was a transient flash. They missed the goodly pearl.

Here is another from the Scriptural gallery of disastrous failures. "Demas has forsaken me, having loved this present evil world." Think of that man's opportunity! He had the privilege of the fellowship of the Apostle Paul, but he "loved the garish day," and he preferred glamour to serenity and a loud sensation to an ideal friendship. The world offered a Bohemian hour, and he took it, and the end thereof was found in. the white, cold ashes of moral defeat. Thus life is frittered away on a thousand trifles, and at the end of the restless quest we have no pearls.

Now the big things of life belong to the realm of spirit and character. It is in the region of the soul that we find the pearls. The really goodly things, the big things, are inside and not outside the man. The big thing is not luxury, but contentment; not a big house, but a big satisfaction; not accumulated art treasures, but a fine, artistic appreciation; not a big library, but a serene studiousness; not a big estate, but a large vision. The big things are not "the things that are seen, but the things that are not seen." "Seek peace and ensue it." "Seek the things that are above." "Seek ye first the Kingdom of God and His righteousness." Such are the goodly pearls.

But the quest of the kingly man is not only for the big things--it is for the bigger things among the big, and for the biggest among them all. The merchantman was not only in search of goodly pearls; he discriminated among the values of pearls, and he knew when he had found "one pearl of great price." There are gradations of value even among good things. There are pearls and better pearls, and the true king in life is known by his pursuit of the best. Knowledge is a good thing, the mastery of the secrets of the visible world; wisdom is a better thing, the possession of fine judgment and delicate intuition, of moral and spiritual discernment. Acquaintance is a good thing; friendship is a better thing; love is the best thing. The respect of others is a good thing; self-respect is a better thing; a fine, untroubled conscience is the best thing. Love for our lovers is a good thing; love for our neighbours is a better thing; love for our enemies is the best thing. There are pearls and there are pearls of great price. And so this, I say, is a mark of the children of the kingdom. They are always in quest of something beyond. "Not as though I had already attained, either were already perfect, but I press on." There is ever a height beyond, a better pearl still to win. "Glories upon glories hath our God prepared, by the souls that love Him one day to be shared." Such is the aim of the kingly quest. It is in search of the goodliest among the goodly pearls.

Now let us look at the quality of the quest. A kingly man is "like unto a merchantman." So the pearls are not found by the loafer, by the mere strolling fiddler along life's way. We are to have the characteristics of business men, even when we are engaged in the affairs of the Highest. If only we assume that requirement as an essential condition of the Kingdom of Heaven, a thousand religious failures will be at once explained. The majority of us are about as little like merchantmen in our religious life as could be very well conceived. And yet this is the Master's demand. We are to be business-like in our search for pearls. And if we are to be business-like what will be some of our characteristics?

First of all, we shall have breadth of outlook. A good merchant has an eye for new markets, for fresh opportunities in new fields. He watches drifts and tendencies, movements of population, and he is the alert friend of every new discovery. His eyes roam over wide areas in quest of new openings to push his trade. And so it is in the Kingdom of Heaven. The man of the kingly life must seek his pearls in many markets and over wide fields. He must seek them in worship and in prayer and in praise. He must look for them in the crowded places of human fellowship. He must search the wide expanse of literature. He must busy himself with the treasures of history. He must be curious in the bright domain of wit and humour. He must be wakeful even on the battlefield, when he is in combat with hostile forces, as well as in the quieter places of human service and communion. He must assume that anywhere and everywhere he may find a goodly pearl. So he must have an eye for markets at every hour of the day and amid all the change and varieties of human experience. This he must do if he would be a "merchantman seeking goodly pearls."

And, secondly, he must have the ability to fix attention on details. The vision of a merchantman is not only telescopic, it is microscopic. "He lets nothing escape him." He knows the weight and force of apparent nothings; he knows the value of seeming trifles. He often finds his treasure in things that other men despise or throw away. He is very inquisitive when he finds apparent waste, if by chance he may turn it into gold. So must it be in the quest for the goodly pearls of the Kingdom. We must give keen attention to the neglected trifles of life. Lowly duties must be carefully scanned. Small disappointments must be examined as though they were dark caskets containing possible treasure. Even commonplace courtesies must not be scouted, but must be regarded as a possible hiding place of priceless gems. The Master Himself described the man of fine quest as being "faithful in that which is least." He does little things in a great way, and he makes great discoveries in doing them.

Thirdly, the kingly life must be distinguished by method and order. A fine business man must have method in his work. He has not only principles, he has rules; he has not only a general system, he has a detailed order. Men who have no method are soon compelled to close their doors. And so it is in the life of the Kingdom of Heaven. We do not stroll carelessly up to the pearls and find them in some haphazard and vagrant loitering. No man lounges into any treasure that is worth having. And that is why so many of us are very poor in the things of the Kingdom. We have no order and method, and the work of one hour is undone by the hour that succeeds it. Look at our prayers. How unmethodical and disorderly? Are they likely to find any pearls? Look at our worship. How little intelligent quest is in it! Is it likely to discover any pearls? Look at our service. How careless it often is and how pointless and unprepared! There are abundant signs that even our Lord Himself regulated His life and refused to allow it to frivol away in indefinite purpose and desire.

Lastly, the man in search of goodly pearls must be distinguished by decision. A competent merchantman knows when to act, and at the decisive moment he acts with commanding promptness. He watches circumstances when they are ripening, and at the proper moment he plucks the fruit. There are times in a business man's life when promptness requires great courage. There is a demand for risk and speculation and untried enterprise, and timidity would let the promising circumstance go by and lose its bounty. So is it in the Kingdom of Heaven. Here, too, there are "tides in the affairs of men which, taken at the flood, lead on to fortune." It is a great thing to know when the hour is ripe for decision. It is one of the fine arts of living to know when to act upon an impulse, and when to accept the hints of emotion as the signs of a favouring gale. Here again our Lord is our example. He was very patient, but He was always very decisive. No one could move Him before the appointed time. No one could stop Him when He said, "The hour has come." Such is to be the quality of our quest. We are to be like merchantmen, broad in outlook, vigilant for detail, intelligent in method, and decisive in action.

With such a spirit we shall undoubtedly discover the goodly pearls, and we shall discover the best of all, "the pearl of great price." But for that pearl we may have to sell many others. What are we prepared to give for it? What are we ready to surrender? According to our consecrated enterprise will be our holy gains. If we refuse to part with Mammon we can never possess the Lord. If we contentedly hug the good we can never gain the better. If we take our ease in the realm of the better we can never enter the best. What are we ready to lose for Christ?

Were the whole realm of nature mine,

That were an offering far too small.

Love so amazing, so divine,

Demands my life, my soul, my all.

X. WITHERED HANDS

ALL the miracles of our Lord are purposed to be symbols of analogous works which can be wrought in the soul. "But that ye may know that the Son of Man hath power" to heal and emancipate the spirit He restored a paralyzed body to freedom. He drove the palsy out of the body as a token that He could drive the palsy out of the soul. He could impart the same strength and buoyancy and agility to the one as He had given to the other. And so it is with all the miracles of our Lord; they are types of the "greater things than these" which He can work among the secret needs of the spirit. Here was a man with a withered hand. A legend comes along the centuries that he was a bricklayer, an ordinary working man, who had been reduced to impotence by the loss of the member he needed most. But his calamity had not embittered him or made him spiritually insensitive. He was found in the synagogue seeking communion with God. And there the Master met him and restored life to his withered limb, and he was whole again.

Now there are withered faculties of the soul. There are spiritual members that can become dry and impotent. There are mysterious hands which can lose their grip and even their power to apprehend the heights. And a diseased faculty can impair the strength of the entire life. It can check our spiritual progress, and impair the vigour of moral aspiration and service. And these withered limbs can be found in the Church. They are brought into the place of worship, and they are often taken out again withered and dead. We do not establish the communion with the Healer which insures the ministry of the irresistible forces of grace.

The faculty of love can be a withered hand. It can shrivel away until it has no strength, no reach, no hold. I suppose we may test the quality of love by the length and strength of its apprehension. How far can it stretch? What is the intensity of its grip? How long can it hold out? The people who have the strongest love have the fullest assurance of moral triumph.. It is sometimes said that money can unlock any door. The statement is the merest nonsense. There are treasure-houses, the most real and the best, that money can never touch. Love is the great "open sesame." A man with a fine love burns his way like fervent iron through ice. He pierces through every difficulty, and nothing is allowed to obstruct his way. "Love never faileth." But when the love itself begins to wither, like a limb that shrivels through lack of vitality, life is comparatively impotent. And how frequently we see this spiritual tragedy! "I have something against thee, thou hast lost thy first love." It is the disease of the withered hand. Something has happened at the very fountains of vitality, and love sickens and dies.

The faculty of hope can be like a withered hand. Think for a moment of a man endowed with brilliant hope, pursuing some personal quest or engaged in some social crusade. What power there is in his goings! What spring there is in the feet of a man who "feels the days before him"! The man who lays hold of the triumph of to-morrow has a mighty inspiration in the battle of to-day. The man who sees "the holy city, New Jerusalem, coming down out of heaven from God" is a glorious labourer in the Jerusalem that is, seeking to transform and transfigure it into the light and beauty of his vision. The man endowed with hope is a magnificent worker. He sees the diamond in the carbon; he sees the finished garden in the desert waste. But if hope shrivels into despondency, or dies away in despair, how helpless is the man who touches the task! It is hope that fetches the bread that feeds endeavour; it is hope that sustains the life. We are "saved by hope." But let hope shrivel, and a dulness steals over the spirit; laxity and limpness take possession of the soul. When a man can say, "I have lost my hope," he is a man with a withered hand.

The conscience can be a withered hand. A live conscience gives a man a fine, nervous, sensitive, "feeling" touch of the mind of God. It gives a man a discerning apprehension of right and wrong. When the feeling is really sensitive, what confidence it imparts to life's movements, what firmness, what motion, what decision! But the conscience can be benumbed. It can become as unresponsive as a paralyzed hand. Common experience affords abundant illustration. There are many people who were once endowed with a scrupulous moral sense, and in some way or other it has lost its exquisiteness, and they no longer finely realize the will of God. The withering is made manifest in apparently small disloyalties. We do not sustain the sense of honour in the full round of common life. There are ministers who are intensely scrupulous about orthodoxy who are not equally scrupulous in more practical obligations. They shrink from heresy; they do not shrink from debt. I have known people deface other people's property by writing Scriptural texts upon it! They have a sensitive desire to serve the Lord, but their honour is not keen enough to make them respect the common rights of their fellows. And often the unscrupulous may degenerate into the vicious. Moral unsoundness is like every other disease, it can proceed from the apparent trifle until it corrupts the pillars of the life. Poison can begin with a pin-prick and may at length reach the heart. A withering conscience is an unspeakable peril. A withering conscience indicates that a man is dead.

The will may be like a withered hand. What a strong, pushful, resourceful hand it is when it is endowed with healthy vitality! But when it withers, everything is touched with irresolution and hesitancy. Nothing is initiated with power. Nothing is addressed with persistence. Nothing is accomplished with decision. A feeble will makes all life's doings anaemic. Everything is languid, from the sickly promise to the imperfect achievement.

What can we do with all or any of these faculties of the soul? We have only one resource. We can bring them to Him who made them, and who can remake them by the power of His grace. But we must bring them deliberately, naming the withered member in the presence of our Lord. We must bring them submissively, laying aside all presumption and pride. We must bring them obediently, ready and willing to carry out the King's decrees. If He orders us to attempt the impossible, we must attempt it. "Stretch forth thy hand!" The man might have replied, "Master, that is just what I cannot do!" "Stretch forth thy hand," and the attempt being made, the needful power was found, and the man was made whole. So must I bring my withered love to Him, and if need be I must "stretch it forth" in effort and service. If He bid me I must act as though I have a healthy love, and in the very effort I shall find I have received it. I must bring my withered hope to Him. At His command I must stretch it forth. I must act as a hopeful man, and I shall find that the gracious light is restored. The Saviour's power goes with the Saviour's demand. The Saviour's power is received in human obedience.

XI. THE THORN REMAINS

THE Apostle Paul was afflicted with some bodily infirmity, some extremely painful disease whose symptoms were marked by frequent recurrence. Many suggestions have been made as to the nature of the disease. Bishop Lightfoot inclines to the opinion that it was epilepsy. Others have fixed upon ophthalmia; Ramsay has recently advanced the theory of malarial fever. It does not very much matter for our immediate purpose what was the particular form of the infirmity. Whatever it was, it appeared to cripple the Apostle; his sacred purpose seemed to be hampered and partially defeated. Even the healthiest of bodies would have been all too slow and sluggish for his burningly passionate soul; but a damaged body was an obtrusive impediment to his great crusade. He prayed about it as only Paul could pray; he prayed that it might depart from him. He offered the prayer twice, thrice, and repeatedly. And then there was given to him that mystic revelation, that enlightenment of conscience, that dawning of interpretation, so often given to the soul that waits on God; he was given the wider vision, the larger understanding, in which similar problems find their solution. "My grace is sufficient for thee, for My power is made perfect in weakness." And this being interpreted seems to say, "Thy apparent weakness may be a channel of strength. The seemingly ungracious thing may be a means of grace. The very infirmity of the organ may confirm the authority of the message. God may become more visible through thy frailty. God may dawn upon the world through thy gloom. My grace is sufficient for thee; through thy seeming weakness My power shall be perfected." And so these were the results of the Apostle's prayers; first, the thorn remained, the bodily pain continued as his guest; second, the prayer was answered in an accession of grace which converted a crown of thorns into a crown of glory.

So this seems to be the principle of the interpretation given to the Apostle Paul. The apparent weakness may become the very occasion of power.

The seeming handicap may redound to the glory of the Lord. The combatants seem to be one man with a thorn versus the tremendous resistance of Asia, and the supercilious cynicism and indifference of Athens, Corinth, and Rome. But the realities are these: one man with a thorn plus the grace of God, and the very thorn becomes a medium of power, and through the obtrusive weakness God's strength is more perfectly revealed. When Paul had fully grasped the significance of this enlightenment his impatience was changed into quietness, his irritableness into confidence, and his complaint into sacred jubilation. "Most gladly therefore will I rather glory in my weaknesses, that the strength of Christ may spread a tabernacle over me." "I take pleasure in weaknesses . . . for when I am weak then am I strong."

So here is the vivid lesson shining across the Apostle's consecrated life; he prayed, and yet the thorn remained, but grace was given whereby the very infirmity became the servant of his strength and a minister to the glory of God.

Now let us bring that principle into our own life, and let us see its applications to our own conditions and needs. We too have our thorns in the flesh, things that seem to hinder our work, apparent obstructions to the progress of the Kingdom of God. If these could be taken away, with what blessed freedom we could run in the way of God's commandments! We pray that the hindrance might be taken away from us. And yet it remains, and the meaning of the apparently unanswered prayer is this, that God wishes to give grace in order that these seemingly adverse circumstances may be converted into our slaves, and made to minister to our own highest interests, to the welfare of others, and to the glory of God.

Take the matter of physical frailty. Perhaps that is our trouble. Just the lack of lusty robustness. Our reserves of strength are very scanty. We are hampered by the bodily clog, and the interests of the Kingdom suffer. We pray for the restoration of health, but the thorn remains. But the prayer is not unanswered. God comes to us in an accession of grace which converts the very sword into a ploughshare, into an implement of moral and spiritual culture. Frances Ridley Havergal was very frail, frail as the most delicate porcelain. She prayed for greater strength, but the thorn remained. But who will say that her prayer was unanswered? Think of the tender songs that were sung from her frail tent! Her very weaknesses endowed her with delicacies of intuition, discernments in sacred explorations, sympathies with the travail of her Lord, which have made her the precious guide and teacher of tens of thousands of the children of God. Her power was made perfect in weakness. Or take Mrs. Browning. Physically she was frail as an autumn leaf. "Once I wished not to live, but the faculty of life seems to have sprung up in me again from under the crushing feet of heavy grief." She prayed once, twice, thrice, and the thorn remained. But grace was given, and she gave us "Aurora Leigh" and "The Cry of the Children." "I cannot lament having learned in suffering what I taught in song." Her husband declared that she was "always smilingly happy with a face like a girl's." And when I take down Mrs. Browning's poems I think of her frail and wan face, and those large, serene eyes, and the calm and lofty brow, and I say "His power was made perfect in her weakness."

Or take another apparent infirmity, the affliction we call nervousness. Some people are like a bundle of exposed nerves. They are endowed with exquisiteness of feeling which makes every jar a discord, a catastrophe. They experience vividness and intensity of emotion. They are slim and sprightly, and the crack of the whip almost excites a mental and moral convulsion. They pray for its removal. They ask for a temperament a little more numb to all the pangs of outrageous fortune. But the thorn remains. The prayer is answered in a better way. By the grace of Christ their very sensitiveness is made the minister of strength and fruitful service. God's power is made perfect in weakness. Robertson of Brighton was extremely sensitive. He was easily jarred. His whole being was as full of feeling as the eye. An ugly colour "brought on nervous irritations." "A gloomy day afflicted him like a misfortune." He prayed for the removal of the infirmity, and the thorn remained. But his prayer was answered. His very weakness was made the vehicle of strength. His sensitiveness gave him his sense of awe and triumph in the presence of nature. It gave him his almost instinctive sense of the characters of men. It gave him his superlatively fine apprehension of the secrets of the Most High. His nervous temperament remained, but God gave him a sufficiency of grace, and through his apparent infirmity God's power was made perfect.

And so it is with many other infirmities that one might name. It is true of temptation. It is true of the disposition that is haunted by painful questionings. They may become to us the ministers of God's holy grace. If the thorn were removed one of the helpers of our health and progress would be gone. The thorn on the rose-bush is the purposed friend and not the enemy of the rose. The flower is all the more surely perfected because the thorn remains. And so it is with the thorns of the soul. By the very retention of the thorn faith is nourished, and ordered power, and the faculty to apprehend the glory of God when He is pleased to reveal it. And thus are we led to the all-sufficiency of the grace of the Father in the Heaven.

XII. THE SONG OF MOSES AND THE LAMB

IN the mystical and mysterious book of Revelation there is a strange and jubilant song sung by "them that have gotten the victory over the beast." I am not concerned to identify any particular beast over whom these singers had proved victorious. The beast may very well and justly stand as typical of all that is unspiritual, the general beastliness which man has to encounter as he struggles towards his crown. Tennyson gives me the suggestion I seek in his description of the four tiers of symbolic sculpture which adorned the walls of Merlin's Hall:

On the lowest beasts were slaying men;

On the second men were slaying beasts;

On the third were warriors, perfect men,

And on the fourth were men with growing wings.

The singers in the Seer's vision had attained to this glorious power of wing; they had gotten the victory over the beast.

And what was the burden of their song? First of all they sang the eternal righteousness of God. "Righteous and true are Thy ways." That is ever the main theme of psalmist, prophet, apostle, martyr, and saint; that is the ground-work of the heavenly music, the very stuff and substance of the song. The praise of the blest is not primarily concerned with the tender love of God or His infinite compassion; not first with the flowers of the earth, but with earth's enduring frame; not first with God's graces, but with His grace, His incorruptible holiness. For what love can there be without a basis of truth? And what is the worth of mercy without the solidity of rectitude? And so it is that when these singers break into song this is the theme of their music: "Holy, holy, holy is the Lord!"

And, secondly, their music wanders among the wonders of God's progressive providence. "Great and marvellous are Thy works! "These works are not primarily the works of nature, but the works of grace. The singers are contemplating the truth in its conflict with falsehood. They are watching the wonders of holiness in its hallowing ministries among the children of men. They are recalling the romance of God's providence as they see it unrolled through the generations of their own troubled national history. And their doxology of providence and grace gathers about two names, the names of Moses and the Lamb. In their songful recital of providential deliverances these two names seem to crystallize and tell the story. And what is the significance of the names? Surely it is this: Moses signifies emancipation from social bondage; the Lamb signifies emancipation from spiritual bondage. Moses stands for deliverance from wrong. The Lamb stands for deliverance from sin. Moses delivers from the wrong which man may suffer from his brother. The Lamb delivers from the wrong which man may suffer from himself. Moses delivers from the Pharaoh outside man. The Lamb delivers from the devil within man. Moses delivers from the gall of oppression and pain. The Lamb delivers from the gall of guilt and sin. This is the song the singers sing, the "Song of Moses and the Lamb"--Thy marvellous works in Moses against all wrong; Thy marvellous works in the Lamb against all sin!

Let me still further emphasize the distinction here made. The song of Moses described a deliverance from the Egyptian house of bondage. It narrated an Exodus from oppression and servitude. The deliverance was the destruction of a galling yoke imposed by man on man. It was the overthrow of tyranny. And that deliverance is sung as a great and marvellous work of God; God is working through a human leader to human emancipation. And this deliverance by Moses is being continued to our own day. In every generation there is some new Exodus from servitude, led by men inspired by the Holy Spirit of God. The leader himself may not be conscious of his divine inspiration, but he is nevertheless the instrument of God's right hand. Wherever men have been fettered in physical servitude, wherever minds have been imprisoned in the darkness of ignorance, wherever hearts have been bruised and broken and a leader has appeared to set the captive free, that leader was a Moses, the champion of a new Exodus, and his crusade of freedom was inspired of the Lord.

Our own time has been singularly distinguished by such emancipations. I know not how many big and petty tyrannies have been fought within the compass even of one generation. In mine and factory, among women and children, on land and sea, among the labourers in the field, and among the sailors on the deep, yokes have been broken, prison doors have been opened, oppression has been righted, and captives have been led into the fair domain of freedom. To tell the story of freedom during the last fifty years would be to sing "a Song of Moses" worthy to be chanted with the song of Revelation sung by the victors at the crystal sea.

There are many more bondages yet to be broken; many more tyrants yet to be dethroned. Wrongs still stalk abroad unabashed and unashamed. There is many a chivalrous exodus yet to be won. And the heavenly allies are on the side of those who seek to do the work. The mystic horses and chariots are on the hill. The mystic ministers, with their golden censers and their golden vials, are still in active service. We are fellow-workers with the spirits of good men made perfect, and all heaven is enlisted on the side of those who seek "to set at liberty them that are oppressed."

But when the "Song of Moses" has been sung, what then? Lead your bondslaves out of Egypt. When you have lifted the tyranny, what about those who have been set free? When you have given the seaman the protection of the load-line he may still reel about the port. When you have lifted the tyranny from the factory operative he may delight to be a beast. When you have given the labourer a vote you have not given him either a conscience or a will. The fact of the matter is, when we have lifted a man out of Egypt we may yet leave him in hell. And let it be remembered that a man may remain in the bondage of Egypt, and yet be in heaven. There is many a servant living to-day in severe and unattractive social servitude who is yet in fellowship with a heaven their master or mistress has never known. Slaves sang their songs in the early Christian Church while they were still in their servitude, and we catch snatches of the music to-day. Yes, all that is true; the prison-house has been bright with the splendours of heaven. And this, too, I say, is true; that a man may gain a certain liberty and yet may enter into a deeper servitude. A man may be redeemed from Egypt and may become a more ignoble slave. The shackles may have been struck from his limbs but they are still on his soul. One tyrant is gone, but the greater tyrant remains. What, then, do we need? Moses can destroy the lesser tyranny, but he cannot touch the greater. We need another and a mightier exodus; we need another and a mightier Moses. The one can work the wonders of the Red Sea and smite and cleave the intercepting flood; we need one who can command and subdue the waters of passion and make its turbid waters clear and clean as the crystal sea. And so to the "Song of Moses" it is imperative that we add the "Song of the Lamb." We shall find at Calvary what can never be found at the Red Sea.

"Babylon is fallen." So do I hear again and again resounding in the Book of Revelation. It is the emancipating word of Moses, and we needs must sing and shout when the tyrant is vanquished, "The slave trade is fallen!" It is the emancipating word of Moses, and we needs must sing when the slave is free. But what has happened when we sing the "Song of the Lamb"? Another exodus has happened with deeper experiences, leading into a far more glorious freedom. "If the Son, therefore, shall make you free ye shall be free indeed." And how are His freed ones described? They are "clothed in white robes"; they have attained to purified habits and dispositions. They have "palms in their hands," the symbol of sovereignty, the emblem of a strong and graceful self-conquest and self-control. And they are singing; the discords of life have been subdued to sweetest harmony. Such is the free one in the Lord. Moses can never make him; he is the creation of the Lamb.

There is a very modern significance in all this. It is imperative that we remember that Moses can never do the work of the Lamb. We are living in a day when we are very much tempted to believe he can. The "Song of Moses" is prone to make us forget the "Song of the Lamb." We are busy, and wisely busy, legislating, emancipating, educating, co-operating. It is all good, and I will sing the song of thanksgiving, but it will never do. The Moses-ministry is pathetically insufficient. It may give us a little more ease, it will never give us a wealthy peace. It may make us more comfortable; it will never make us inherently good. "We are complete in Him," in Him alone, and in Him only, "the Lamb slain from the foundation of the world."

XIII. WAVE AND RIVER

I AM writing these words in sight of a fine, fresh sea. A strong south-westerly breeze is blowing, and huge waves are moving swiftly to their culmination, and breaking majestically on the shore. A little way up the coast a broad river, full and brimming, fed by a hundred tributaries from the rain-drenched hills, is leisurely emptying its voluminous flood into the advancing sea. And as my eyes pass from the sea to the river, and again from the river to the sea, I am reminded of two very powerful figures, used by the greatest of the Old Testament prophets, and which may have had their birth in conditions similar to those which I am gazing upon to-day. "O, that thou hadst hearkened to My commandments; then had thy peace been like a river, and thy righteousness like the waves of the sea." The figures are strikingly original and suggestive, and I think that they enshrine conceptions of truth which afford healthy correctives to some soft and effeminate thinking of our own time.

"Then had thy peace been like a river!" That itself is a most unusual sphere in which to find a symbol of peace. Most people, when they want a symbol of peace, would seek it in some secluded mountain-tarn, nestling quiet and unrippled far away from beaten roads, and where even the cry of a vagrant bird is only rarely heard. It is by these "still waters," and in these deep silences, that we should call to mind the gift of peace. Other people are impressed with the "peacefulness" of the chamber of death. When they see the body lying perfectly still, and when every sound is muffled, everybody speaking in whispers, and going about on tiptoe, they feel constrained to say, "How peaceful!"

How different is the prophet's choice of figure! Not a stagnant tarn, not a lifeless body, but a river! The erroneous conception gathers about a particular sort of stillness; the true conception gathers about a particular quality of movement. Peace is not motionless quietness, but quiet motion. Peace has its appropriate figure in the brimming river, deeply quiet because of its depth. Peace is liquid motion, frictionless movement! That is the phrase which expresses my present thought. Perfect peace is found in human life when that life moves in God's life without babble, or fret, or friction. It is not so much found in the absence of sound as in the absence of discord. It is musical movement, it is harmony.

Our Master's conception of peace is given in His oft-repeated words, "I and My Father are one." When one life flows into another life with perfect commingling--will with will, thought with thought, desire with desire, then we have the basal secret of peace. And when that perfect commingling is between the human heart and God, we have learned the secret of perfect peace. That was Jesus's peace, and this is Jesus's promise, "My peace I give unto you."

"And thy righteousness like the waves of the sea." Well, let me go nearer the sea. I leave the dry upper beach, and go down to the water's edge. There in the distance a fine wave is forming, gathering volume and impetus as it rolls. Let me step forward, confront it, and check its advance! The wave laughs at the antagonism, and races shoreward with powerful and jubilant flood. And my righteousness is purposed to be like that! "Thy righteousness like the waves of the sea." But in the lives of the majority of us, even of those who profess to know the Lord, there is nothing characteristic of a glorious wave. Our righteousness is more like some trembling rivulet, uncertainly threading its way in time of drought. Any small antagonism can check it, and delay it, and divert it. We timidly shrink behind the impediment; we do not clear it at a leap! The truth is, the wave-force is pathetically lacking in many Christian lives. There is nothing strong and positive; there is no vigorous trend because there is no definite end. Their purposes meander along, and any obstacle can hinder them, and any hostile foot can turn them aside.

If our life is to find a fitting symbol in the waves of the sea, then it is to be distinguished by a commanding force of character. It will be grandly impressive, and will be known by its "go." Surely, this must be something of the meaning of Paul's inspiring words, "we have not received again the spirit of fear . . . but of power." Ours is not to be a spirit of fear, of trembling, like the uncertain surf, "carried with the wind and tossed" about the shore. Ours is to be a spirit of power, moving in noble impressiveness, and with the invincible majesty of a magnificent wave. Again and again our Lord sets before His disciples the strong ideal of a character which "tells," which is positive and bracing. He seemed to be afraid of their discipleship weakening down into an anaemic sentimentality, a forceless effeminacy which would never arrest the world, or take the Kingdom of Heaven by storm. He did not wish His disciples to be only as a pleasant perfume; He wished them to be more like that strong breeze which is even now blowing upon me from the southwest, pervaded with the pungent smack of the salt sea! "Ye are the salt of the earth." I think it is the same element of impressiveness which is suggested in the figure of the advancing wave. And when this forceful, impressive element is wanting, when this energetic spirit is absent, then the individual Christian, or that fellowship of Christians which we call the Church, becomes as "salt that has lost its savour," a poor, savourless presence, and the world will pay no heed, or treat it as something to be despised and "trodden under foot of men." There were some in the Corinthian Church who had become thus enervated and forceless, and the Apostle seeks to stir them up into a more vigorous life. "Some are sickly, and not a few sleep!" How far was this from the forcefulness of the triumphant wave! It was more significant of the stagnant pool, with a noisome corruption mantling its idle face. There are many men who, on the business side of their life, have all the strong impetuosity of a wave but on the distinctively moral and religious side their will beats as feebly as a forceless pulse. They flaunt a religious profession, but they have no religious "life." These constitute the very bane of the Kingdom, for they are the unimpressive professionals who make the Christian religion unattractive and repellent. But when our righteousness becomes like a wave, its very power will hold the world in rich and fertile wonder.

XIV. THE GUIDING HAND

THERE is a familiar phrase which is twice repeated in the twenty-third Psalm: "He leadeth me," but the two usages have very different surroundings. In the first the surroundings are pastoral, a deep restfulness is in the air, and all things are significant of relaxation and repose. "He leadeth me beside waters of rest." It is like walking on the banks of a river on some serene Saturday night, when the work of the week is over, and the very beasts of the field seem to have begun their Sabbath rest. In the second usage the surroundings are altogether changed. Rest becomes action; relaxation becomes strenuousness. We leave the "waters of rest" for the exposed and storm-swept uplands. We turn to the frowning slopes, with their terrors of wild beasts and tempests. Life becomes militant. "He leadeth me in the paths of righteousness." It is like leaving the sweet and fragrant vineyards of the lower Alpine slopes for the bare and craggy heights, and the dubious and treacherous ways of the snow. But the guide who leads through the vineyard leads also through the snows; and it is the same God who leads by the "waters of rest," who also leads into exacting and exhausting "ways of righteousness." The Lord of the restful valley is also King of the flood and Sovereign of the terrible heights.

And this brings me to the theme of the present meditation; the Divine leadership, the grace of the guiding hand. There is surely nothing remote or obscure in the theme. It is relevant and immediate to everybody. We differ in many things and in many ways; we differ in age and in calling, in physical fitness and in mental equipment; we differ in knowledge and accomplishments; we are greatly different in temperament, and therefore in the character of our daily strife. But in one thing we are all alike--we are pilgrims travelling between life and death, on an unknown road, not knowing how or when the road may turn; not knowing how or when it may end; and we are in urgent need of a Greatheart who is acquainted with

70

every step of the way. We are all in need of a leader who will be our guide by the "waters of rest," and also in the perilous ways of the heights.

Now how does the Lord lead us? I want to find the answer in the word and life of the Scriptures. And when I turn to the Scriptures I find that the means and methods of Divine leadership are many, that the Great Leader is like a wise human leader, and He adapts His ministries to the nature of the child and the character of the immediate need. I can only mention two or three of these varied methods of leadership as I find them in the Word of God.

And here is the first: "And the Lord spoke thus to me with a strong hand." It is the speech of a young prophet, and it describes a leading of God. Let us apprehend the figure. The counsel of the Lord has come to Isaiah like a strong hand, as something he could not escape. The intuition laid hold upon him like an arrest. What was the nature of the counsel? He was called upon by the Lord to separate himself from his nation. by a solemn act of detachment. He was commanded to confront his people, to oppose them, to leave the majority and stand alone. He was bidden to prophesy the unpleasant and even to predict defeat. We know how such men are regarded--they are denounced as unpatriotic, as devoid of national feeling and fraternal ambition. The young prophet shrinks from the task; he is tempted to silence and retirement; he meditates retreat; but the Word of the Lord came to him "with a strong hand." The imperative gave him no freedom; heaven laid hold on him with holy violence; the invisible gripped his conscience as a man's arm might be gripped, until it ached in the grasp.

Now this is one method of leading--a grip like that of a powerful constable. This was the kind of leading that came to Saul as he journeyed to Damascus. It was the kind of violent arrest that laid hold of John Bunyan as he played on Elstow-green. Sometimes the violent leading takes the shape of a startling ministry of disappointment or affliction. Sometimes the

Lord lays hold of us with the cold, stony grip of fear, and we are moved in the way of life by the terror of impending calamity. Yes, the holy Lord sometimes arises and "shaketh terribly the earth." He grips and He shakes; but the ministry is governed by infinite mercy and love. "By terrible things in righteousness dost Thou answer us, O God of our salvation."

And here is a second method of leading: "I will guide thee with Mine eye." How startling the change! We pass from the grip of the hand to the glance of an eye, from a grip as severe as a vise to a touch as gentle as light. We pass from a nipping frost to a soft and cheering sunbeam. I find the word in the thirty-second Psalm, and the Psalm itself has provided me with the figure of violent contrast. "Be ye not as the horse or the mule." The mule is headlong and headstrong, and he is to be guided by the "strong hand." But the Lord would guide us by His eye. How exceedingly delicate is the guidance of a look! What tender intercourse can pass through the eyes! There is a whole language in their silent communion. But let it be marked that this eye-guidance implies very intimate fellowship. Eye-speech is the speech of lovers. We may be guided by a "strong hand," even when we are heedless of God; we can only be guided by His eye when we are gazing on God.

Let me give two examples of lovers who were guided by the eye. And let this be the first: "They looked unto Him and were lightened." That is guidance by a look. Whilst they worshipped they received the light. Their minds were illumined while they gazed. "They caught the ways of God," and they had a certain radiance of spirit which assured them that they had found the King's will. We cannot say much about the delicate experience through the clumsy medium of words. There are some communions for which ordinary language is altogether insufficient. Who can explain the message that passed between souls in love with one another; and who can . describe the gentle communion of souls in love with God?

But here is another instance of this delicate guidance of the eye: "Jesus turned and looked upon Peter." That, too, was a look from Lover to lover. I know that one of the lovers had failed, but his love was not quenched. He had failed at the test, but the love was still burning. And Jesus turned, and with a look of poignant anguish He led His disloyal disciple into tears, and penitence, and reconciliation, and humble communion, and liberty. Peter was guided by the eye of his Lord.

Let me give one further instance of the leadings of God, and this time from the experience of the Apostle Paul: "After they were come to Mysia they assayed to go into Bithynia, but the Spirit suffered them not." And what kind of leading was this? It was leading by impediment. It was guidance by prohibition. It was the ministry of the closed door. There came to the Apostle what the Friends would describe as a "stop in the mind." His thought was resisted and had no liberty. He felt that his purpose was secretly opposed by an invincible barrier. In certain directions he had no sense of spiritual freedom, and therefore he regarded that way as blocked. "The angel of the Lord stood in the way for an adversary." I think it is very needful to emphasize this. God sometimes leads us by negations. The closed door is the indication of His will. We assay to go, but the Spirit suffers us not.

But whatever form the Divine leading may take, it is not always clear and immediate. Our great Leader sometimes keeps us waiting before we know His will. It is often very difficult to find out what His will really is. Would it be well for it to be otherwise? Would it be best for His will to be known immediately, and without the faintest shadow of doubt? Is there no kindly purpose in obscurity? Has mystery no place in the curriculum of life's school? Is there no gracious ministry in delay? If we always and everywhere enjoyed perfect and immediate lucidity we should abide in the condition of babes. We gain immense wealth from the discipline of uncertainty. Uncertainty impels us to exercise our sight. We critically observe the issues. We estimate possibilities. We weigh scruples. If the scales of guidance always went down with a bang it might make it easy, but it would never make us strong. The scales of guidance often turn with a hair, and part of life's discipline consists in watching the scales to see how they turn. The consequence is that when we know God's will we have also strengthened our sight. We have refined our powers of discernment in the act of making the discovery. And as we gain from the discipline of watching we also gain from the discipline of waiting. We gain self-control and patience and the noble refinements of hope. And thus we see that obscurity and delay do not imply the Divine absence or indifference. The Divine Leader is at work, and His gracious purpose is active even in the apparent inaction.

XV. THE MIDNIGHT PRESSURE

THERE is something very weird and haunting about the midnight. It is one thing to be called out to visit the sick at noontide, but there is something awful when the call comes at the midnight. A telegram at the noon may be something or nothing, but a telegram in the stillness of the midnight is startling. And so we use the midnight as the symbol of our deepest and most desolate need. The majority of us have had experience of the season. The lights have gone out, and the soft, genial breeze has changed into a nipping night wind, and there is no companionable sound in the streets. We feel lonely and desolate and cold. And yet God's saints have had some wonderful happenings in the midnight. "Which of you shall have a friend and shall go unto him at midnight?" And countless numbers have turned to the heavenly Friend, and they have found wonderful light and provision in His presence. The Word of the Lord is full of song rising from the hearts of those whose night time has been changed into morning through their communion with the heavenly Friend. Here is a little chorus of praises: "Thou hast visited me in the night"; "In the night His song shall be with me"; "At midnight I will arise and give thanks"; "At midnight Paul and Silas prayed and sang praises." All these pilgrims of the night felt the pressure of the cold loneliness and they were driven to the heavenly Refuge and found the grace of God.

But the very parable from which I have taken this sentence about the visit of the friend in the midnight seems to suggest that God may delay His bounty and that importunity is needed if we are to obtain His aid. Looked at superficially it would seem that the all-comfortable and self-engrossed friend was unwilling to arise from bed and give the loaves that were asked by the shameless knocker at the door. But the teaching is rather this: if continued knocking can overcome the surliness of a well-bedded friend, what will it accomplish when the Friend is the ever-ready, all-compassionate, and sleepless Lord? If continued prayer can overcome reluctance, how will it fare when it deals with goodwill? It is one of the "how much more "arguments of Jesus Christ. If your friend, snugly ensconced in his bed, and unwilling to go out in the cold night, and angry at being disturbed, will at length respond to your importunate knocking, "how much more shall your Father which is in heaven!" And, therefore, we are bidden to ask and to go on asking, to knock and to go on knocking, and the desires of our heart shall be satisfied.

Why should there be any delay at all? Why does not God answer the first knock? First of all, let us again repeat the good news that our God is never imprisoned in sleepy indifference. He is awake and willing before we knock at all. Why, then, should we have to knock again? What is He doing? He is preparing the answer. There are some things we ask for that have to be grown. They cannot be given to us like coins or manufactured goods! They could only be given as fruits and they have to be grown in our souls. We ask for a fruit and the Lord immediately answers our prayer by planting a seed. We may think the prayer is unanswered, while all the time the answer is already working in our life towards consummation. We ask for certain blooms of finished character. The Lord does not attach them to our lives as we might tie fruit to a sickly tree. He begins at once to enrich the character that creates the blooms. For instance, I ask for joy. I expect to receive an immediate ecstasy. I ask the second time, but it does not come. My heart is sad in the midnight and there is no speedy transformation. But that does not mean that my Friend is indifferent or indolent. I ask for joy and He begins to make me a little purer and more refined. He works upon the strings of my soul and endows them with more sensitiveness, and by the preparation of the instrument He will prepare me for the final music and song. I ask for perfect peace. It does not come with the first asking, but the answer begins as soon as I knock at the door. There are broken cogs in the life that have to be repaired. There is much gravel of sin that has to be removed. And if the Lord is repairing some cog or cleaning some wheel, is not this the answer which will bring the peace for which I pray? It may be said that in order to give peace He may have to give pain. The resetting of a joint may mean the temporary increase of my suffering, but God is directing the process which will issue in blessing. But why keep on knocking, knocking; why keep on praying, praying? Why be importunate? Because importunity provides the atmosphere in which implanted seeds become matured. In prayer I receive the seed. By prayer I shall receive the fruit. Men ought always to pray, and the seeds will not faint.

One thing must be added. Sometimes the Lord's answer has really come, but we have not prayed for eyes to see it. It has not come quite in the dress we expected, and, therefore, we did not know it. A friend was appointed to meet me at a railway station. He looked for a man in clerical attire, and we wandered about little knowing that we were brushing shoulders with each other all the time. He thought I had not arrived, but I was there in another dress. And, therefore, it is well to look at our ordinary circumstances when they do not come to us in familiar and expected guise. "He was in the world and the world knew Him not." God sometimes appears in these unexpected ways, but they are the very answers to our prayers. The Apostle Paul was cast down in Macedonia. "Without were fightings, within were fears." And the comfort came in a strange way. It was not given in some immediate lighting of the fires of joy, by some mysterious gift in his secret soul. "The Lord comforted me by the coming of Titus." That is where Paul found the answer to his prayers. A fellow-man came to share his burden and to enhance his joys.

XVI. CAPITAL AND INTEREST

LIFE is very commonly regarded from the standpoint of an investment of capital which yields a certain amount of interest. It was conceived in this figure by the Lord Jesus Himself. "Trade ye herewith till I come." And what is our capital? What capital did the Master Himself invest in the affairs of men? He had a capital of thought, and He invested it in thoughtfulness. He had a capital of emotion, and He invested it in widest sympathy. He had a capital of conscience and ideal, and He invested them in the exploration and correction of crookedness. And He had a capital of will, and He always invested its power in the ministry of rectitude and truth. This was the sort of capital with which Jesus traded, and this is the kind of capital with which we are to trade amid the new opportunities of our own life.

Now, in these realms interest is in proportion to the amount of capital we invest. Small investment will yield but small returns; if the investment be increased the interest will be correspondingly enlarged. Carelessness in the employment of life's capital results in dwindling and exhausted returns. This teaching applies to all kinds of interest, even that interest which we call our interest in things, our interest in persons, in causes, in common affairs. The interest we get from them depends upon the capital we put into them. And here I come face to face with a common statement which I desire to challenge, and which, indeed, is the theme of this meditation. Here is a man speaking about something or other, maybe a society, or a cause, or an institution, and he says, "I began to lose interest in it, and so I gave it up." Now I think the contrary is more likely to have been the truth. A close investigation will rather reveal that the man had begun to give it up and then lost interest in it. There was first an interference with the capital, and then the interest suffered. There was a relaxing in the trade, followed by impaired returns. This may appear to be a subtle, but it is a very vital distinction. The condition of finding interest in anything is the persistent and diligent application of strength. We begin to give a thing up, and then we lose our interest in it.

We may find the application of the principle in the #230;sthetic realm. What is the condition of retaining a keen interest in music? It is the maintenance of an investment of capital. If we add to capital we assuredly add to the interest. The devotion of more time, more thought, more eager listening, and more diligent persistence, will result in an enriched and enlarged commerce, and the genius of music will pour her treasures into our souls. Charles Darwin ceased to invest in this realm; he gave no thought nor attention to music, and so he lost the power of appreciation.

It is even so in the realm of art. The men who get most out of it are the men who put most into it. When John Ruskin began to examine the papers of Turner, he found at least twenty thousand slips, upon which the great artist had sketched all manner of initial themes. He was investing in ideas, and we have the results in his marvellous productions. Ruskin himself is an example of the same simple and universal law. In his preface to Mr. E. T. Cooke's "Guide to the National Gallery," he writes these words: "When I last lingered in the gallery before my old favourites, I thought them more wonderful than ever before." He was continually giving the strength of a finer quest, and he returned from his quest with richer discoveries.

We may follow the application of the principle into the social realm. Even on the elementary plane of a subscription our interest is really born with our contribution. It is surprising what a little investment of this kind will do to create and quicken a man's attention. And if we increase our capital, our interest in the institution increases with it. If we begin to withdraw our contribution, the interest itself is withdrawn. In all social causes our humane interests are in precise proportion to our investments. If we put no thought into the condition of the inhabitants of the Congo, if we send no exploring sympathies among the downtrodden people of Russian cities and Russian wastes, there will be no interest, and these fellow-men will be as though they. had no place on the planet; but if we fix our thoughts upon their oppressions, and their woes, and their deprivations, if we settle our minds upon them, like invested capital, a great interest will waken in our souls, which will again expend itself in chivalrous endeavour and service.

If we .ascend still higher into the affectional realm, into the home of holy love, we shall find that the gracious interest is determined by the quality of our investment. It is even so in the sacred relationship of husband and wife. The love of courtship is often larger and fuller than the love of married life, and it is simply because in the courtship there were more kindly courtesies and more reverent and constant devotion. It frequently happens that, when the wedded life begins, the delicate courtesies that prevailed before the. wedding are dropped, and life becomes grey and conventional. All of which means that capital has been withdrawn and the returns have suffered. Everybody knows how true this is in the relationship of friend and friend. If the capital of thoughtfulness is withdrawn, fraternal interest begins to drop. If two friends become divided by the waste of waters, it may chance that their letters become less and less frequent, and their courtesies more and more scanty, until the old profound, vital interest is almost dead. We begin to give up the friendship, and then the interest dies.

And in the last place, the principle finds application in the highest of all regions, the spiritual realm. Many of us have so little interest in the things of the highest because we put no capital into them. We know perfectly well that if we put as little into anything else, say, into our business, or even into our pleasures, we should have no returns. Take the interest we derive from the Word of God. What right have many of us to expect any interest at all? We put nothing into it, and yet sometimes we expect an abundant return. We do not seek it as we should search for secret veins of gold; we do not diligently seek for it as for "treasure hid in the field." What have we invested in the New Testament? How much of thought, how much of imagination, how much of sympathy, how much of sheer will? From the standpoint of common trade, have we any right to expect returns?

And I would include in all this meditation the means and ministry of prayer. Our interest in prayer is determined by the capital we invest. Look at the example of our Lord the Christ. "Rising a great while before day, He went up into a mountain apart, to pray." "He continued all night in prayer to God." "And as He prayed His sweat was as it were great drops of blood." Has our season of prayer any resemblance to these? Does it suggest energy and sacrifice, even to the point of blood? Are our intercessions weighted with purpose, and have we the demeanour of an armed man cleaving his way to some shining palace of gold? How much do we put into it? When a man speaks of losing interest in prayer, he had better raise the previous question as to the amount of capital he has withdrawn from the holy trade.

Many of us have scarcely begun to pray at all. We have only played at praying. It has not been a mighty business; it has only been a harmless convention. We have put nothing into it, and therefore we have taken nothing out. We have "prayed amiss."

Our primary concern must be with the capital, and God will attend to the interest. Let us invest, in all high and holy things, all our mind and soul and heart and strength. And there will be returned to us in holy interest and affection "good measure, pressed down, shaken together, and running over."

XVII. BRUISED REEDS

THE Scriptures speak of some people under the figure of "bruised reeds." What is the significance of the figure? Think of it, first of all, as a broken musical reed. The shepherd boy cut a reed and turned it into a flute; and sweet music was reed music, mingling with the sound of the breeze on the uplands of the hills, and with the murmur of the pines! But if the reed were bruised and broken, if some beast had stepped upon it with heavy, heedless foot, and it lay there splintered and riven, how worthless the instrument! What shall the shepherd boy do with the reed that has lost its power to make a musical note? He will snap it and fling it away! He will "break the bruised reed."

Now, there are men and women who are just like these broken natural flutes. They have lost the simple music of a sweet and human life. When their souls are breathed upon by the breath of God they are like a splintered reed, and they give no musical response. The breath wakes no bird-note of faith or hope or love. When their souls are breathed upon by the breath of human fellowship they are like a bruised reed, and there is no fraternal answer. They have lost their humanness, their rich, full sympathy with God and man.

How do the reeds become broken? There are many ways in which the fracture may be made. The reed may be broken by the brutal tread of personal sin. A beast going down to the river to slake his thirst may crush a reed into the mire, and an appetite going out to drink may destroy the music of the soul. But the reed can also be broken by the heavy burden of grief and sorrow. We speak of a broken heart, a heart in which the singing spirit is bruised and silent. It is not uncommon, when some heavy calamity of woe has fallen upon a woman, to hear it said of her, "No one ever heard her sing again." The fragile reed was bruised and splintered.

And again, the reed can be fractured by the nipping pressure of anxiety and care. The frost can crack a lute, and freezing care can chill "the genial currents of the soul," and break its music. "How can we sing the Lord's song in the land of the stranger," in a cold climate, where the soul-instrument becomes mute? In all these ways and in many others the fragile reeds can be bruised, and "the daughters of music are brought low."

And what can we do with these "bruised reeds"? I will ask a larger question, in order to obtain a more heartening reply. What will the Saviour do with these "bruised lutes"? Well, He will not break them and finish their destruction. He will not discard and abandon them. He will not fling them away. He will restore the bruised reed. May we not say that He is the Physician of Broken Reeds, going about to restore the lost power of music and song? Unlike the shepherd boy, the Great Shepherd can mend the broken lutes. He can restore unto us "the joy of His salvation." Here is a familiar example. There is a lad with a life yielding a note like the mellow music of a fine, strong, musical reeds His life is whole and melodious, and no beast strides across his sacred place. And then some alien impulse lays hold of him, and he goes forth to "spend his substance in riotous living." The lute is sorely bruised. "He began to be in want." And how was he regarded by his fellows? "No man gave unto him." He was broken and rejected, broken and flung away! But let me hasten to the end of the narrative. "When the elder son came near the house he heard music." And what was that music? It was the restored music of the repaired lute, the love-song sounding again through the mended reed. "He hath put a new song in my mouth." It was the recovery of the lost chord. Thus our gracious Lord can deal with bruised reeds when they have been riven by sorrow or care or sin. "I will seek again that which was lost, and bring again that which was driven away, and will bind up that which was broken, and will strengthen that which was sick."

But we may look again at the figure of the reed in the interpreting light of our Lord. Let us drop the suggestion of the musical reed, and regard it as just the swaying, pliable reed of .the desert. I think there may have been some proverbial phrase associated with the reed of the wilderness, and I think we catch a suggestion of it in the speech of our Lord. "What went ye out into the wilderness to see? A reed shaken by the wind?" The reed of the wilderness was used to describe a certain type and quality of life. The desert reed yielded before the wind; it was swayed, anyhow, any way, anywhere. It bent before the wind, from whatever quarter it blew, and became the type of frailty, fragility, pliability. But we are to add another characteristic even to this vivid symbol of impotence. It is not only a swaying, desert reed, but a "bruised reed," broken on its stem and withering at the fracture! Can we find an image more extraordinarily expressive of concentrated weakness?

Well, now, there are people just like those desert reeds. They are the opportunists, yielding and bruised. They change their opinion every hour, until the very power of conviction is gone. They change their movements with the movements of the hour, until the very power of self-initiative is lost. They become bruised in the wind. What can we do with them? What do we do with them? In our folly we discard them. We despise them. We count them as worthless. We fling them away. But what will the Saviour do with human reeds, these playthings of the wind, the sport of caprice, the broken creatures of the passing hour? "He will not break the bruised reed." He will turn the bruised reed into "an iron pillar," and "out of weakness it shall be made strong."

Here is a man "driven by the wind and tossed." It was said unto him, "Thou also wast with Jesus of Nazareth," but he denied, saying, "I know not, neither understand I what thou sayest." A poor bruised reed, yielding and breaking before the wind! But now listen to the risen Lord. "Go, tell My disciples and Peter." What is the significance of that word? It is the Lord at work on the bruised reed. "Simon, son of Jonas, lovest thou Me?" It is the Lord at work on a broken heart, giving it the gracious opportunity of recovery and of once again expressing itself in adoration and service. Look further on in the narrative. "When they saw the boldness of Peter." And what is the significance of that? It is the old, trembling, shaking reed converted into an iron pillar; it is discipleship made "faithful unto death."

XVIII. INFIRMITIES IN PRAYER

I WANT to consider some of the weaknesses which beset us when we commune with God in prayer. If we can clearly recognize our infirmities we may apprehend what is the promised ministry of the Holy Spirit. "The Spirit also helpeth our infirmities." I know I cannot go far along the road, for it soon passes into mystery and obscurity. But steadily to contemplate our weaknesses will surely reveal to us where the Holy Spirit will bring us needful strength. And in the enumeration of some of these infirmities I think I should first of all mention the weakness of appetite. We may realize this weakness if we contrast it with the strength of appetite revealed in other relationships. Take a man's appetite for business with all its keenness of strenuousness and intensity. Or take a man's appetite for pleasure, which is often as burning as the thirst of the fever-stricken. Or contrast our appetite for a novel with our interest in the things of God. When we turn to pray there is frequently no effective driving taste in our fellowship. And the taste for a thing is always a mighty dynamic. When our taste for anything is weak we loiter along the road, and we are oppressed with our own. weakness. So it is with our weakness of appetite in prayer. We are oppressed by comparative indifference, and in the sense of insipidity we play with the great concern.

And there is a second infirmity which I will call our weakness of faith. We have no strong belief in our business. Real faith is a fountain of boundless energy. At Tobermory, on the west of Scotland, a little handful of men have a strong faith that a sunken galleon from the Spanish Armada is the prison house of great treasure, and their faith is productive of an energy which makes zealous quest. "Faith is the assurance of things hoped for." Faith acts mightily on the assumption that the thing hoped for is, and that the next step may bring us face to face with our goal. Have we this kind of faith? When we turn to God in prayer, do we turn to it with the quiet assurance that we are drawing near to a boundless treasury? Do we set

86

about it as though our hands were upon mighty levers whose movement can effect a revolution? King George touched an electric button in London, and a gate swung open in Canada. A lever was turned in London and a Government House in Cape Town was flooded with light. When we pray to the Lord, does any analogous possibility thrill our souls? Have we faith that we can open closed doors, or that we can be the ministers of enlightenment even to souls that are far away? Surely one of our infirmities is our weakness of faith. We are not uplifted by the assurance that we are in touch with the possibilities of endless possessions.

Another infirmity which I will name is the weakness of spirituality. Even when we go to the treasury we frequently ask for the smallest things. We do not honour the great God by the greatness of our quests. "We ask amiss." Suppose that I were to be admitted into a great library, and I were to be taken around by the owner and reader of the books, and suppose he pointed out to me their wealth of glorious lore, and the wonders of music, of vision, and of dream which they enshrined, and suppose he were to say to me, "Take whatever you like from my library," and I were to choose a wastepaper basket! Would not my request disparage the owner, and trifle with the wealth of his provision? Or if in some great studio the artist himself should point out to me the riches of perception, and the glory of workmanship in line and colour, and he were to offer me anything I pleased to choose, and suppose I were to carry away a picture-frame! But occasions that would be incredible in human relationships are quite common in our relationships with God. We ask Him for things that matter least. We neglect the things that are all-important. We emphasize the temporal rather than the eternal. We choose the earthly instead of the heavenly. We emphasize goods more than goodness, and we are more concerned with bodily health than with spiritual robustness. And all the time the big things are waiting, "above all that we can ask or think."

And here is another of our infirmities when we seek to commune with God, our weakness of sympathy. There is little range in our intercessions. The liners on the high seas can now be contrasted by the wealth of their wireless equipments. Some equipments can only carry correspondence over exceedingly limited areas, while the greatest liners throw their mystic arms over enormous seas. A man's sympathies may be regarded as his wireless equipment. Some are pathetically poor and have no range beyond the circle of their own family life. Others may be sensitive ever the area of their own denomination. But powerful saints have an equipment which touches the joys and sorrows of the uttermost parts of the earth. Our prayers are determined in their range by the wealth or poverty of this equipment, and I think we may say that very commonly our sympathetic correspondences are dwarfed and scanty.

And the last infirmity that I will mention is the weakness of understanding. Frequently when I pray I am face to face with problems to which I can see no solution. We cannot see all round the thing, and we "know not what to pray for as we ought." I am writing these words in the critical hours of the Balkan crisis. Just precisely how shall I pray about it? What would be best for Europe? What redistribution of powers will redound most to the glory of God? Here my understanding may be limited, and I pray without the requisite enlightenment. Well, in all these ways the spirit is encumbered by infirmity, and we are in great need of a mighty Helper. "The Spirit also helpeth our infirmities," and most assuredly He helps us in the midst of all the weaknesses of an enemy. Wherever the soul stumbles in its frailties, the Holy Spirit, if we permit Him, will bring the needful help.

But more than all this I feel sure that the Holy Spirit strengthens the very prayers we make. For what weak things they are, even at the best! Perhaps my body is itself a hindrance. I have a hard day's work, and I am tired out, and I have scarcely the physical or mental vigour to fix my thoughts upon the Highest. My evening prayer is very weak, and has little promise of effectiveness. But surely just here the Holy Spirit will help my infirmities by adding strength to my petitions! Some signatures change weak appeals into conquests. If we can only secure the signature of a member of the Royal house, what urgency it gives to our plea! And perhaps in the mysterious depths of the soul our poor lame appeals receive the signature of the Holy Spirit, and He "maketh intercessions for us with groanings that cannot be uttered."

And, finally, I think the Holy Spirit corrects our prayers. We may pray in our shortsightedness, and we ask the things that will bring no blessing. But the Holy Spirit, who knoweth the mind of God, puts aside our own petition and intercedes for what will bring us the gift of God's wonderful grace. The Apostle Paul prayed that he might be delivered from his "thorn in the flesh," but the Holy Spirit interceded for him, and while the thorn remained he received an all-sufficient endowment of the grace of God. And St. Monica, the mother of Augustine, prayed that her son might not be taken from her side. But the Holy Spirit interceded, and Augustine was taken to Italy, to Milan, to Ambrose, and to his life in Christ!

And thus are we saved from the peril of our own limitations, and better things are given to us than we desired. Our Friend in Communion watches our interests rather than our words, and the gracious answer that comes to us is inspired by His understanding of all things, "yea, of the deep things of God."

XIX. THE FRIENDS OF JESUS

I SUPPOSE that the greatest title ever conferred upon men was the one used by Jesus when He addressed His disciples as "My friends." Compared with this all other titles and nobilities are tawdry and artificial. They are as wax flowers and fruits in contrast with the sweet-perfumed loveliness of gardens and woods. They are like harsh, glaring stage effects set in contrast with the soft splendours of the dawn. An earthly dignity always carries with it a certain autumnal air, a suggestion of the fading leaf. The heavenly dignity is always significant of the eternal spring and the "never-withering flowers." "My friends." No other honour will ever come our way which for a moment can be compared with this.

Let us for a, moment think who He is who confers the title. He is the "young Prince of Glory," the true expression and the subdued effulgence of God. These are familiar and perhaps well-worn words, and their sovereign superscription may have been partially effaced. Does it still awake the sense of wonder that the Prince of Glory walked the dusty ways of men? I remember reading years ago a quaint little book, written with daring and yet reverent imagination, in which the writer sought to express something of the limitless wonder of the angels when the Prince of Glory declared His purpose to leave the abode of light and enter the shadows and the darkness, that He might redeem the stricken earth-family from their sin. The imagination was certainly daring, but the awed spirit of the writer saved it from transgression, and he certainly conveyed some sense of the wondrous happenings in the unseen world when the beloved Prince set out to befriend the children of men. "The word was with God, and the word was God. All things were made by Him, and without Him was not anything made that hath been made." "He is before all things, and in Him all things consist." And this strong Son of God came to befriend the sons and daughters of men, and to seek their friendship in return. "Ye are My friends."

And upon whom does He confer the title? Well, there is a couple of fishermen among them, James and John. He found them on the shore mending their nets. And there are two other fishermen, Simon and Andrew, also found at their humble toil. And there is at least one tax-collector, picked up at the very booth where the customs' dues were being paid. And there is another man, quiet, deep, and thoughtful, discovered in hungry reveries beneath a fig-tree. And these are types of the men the Prince of Glory gathered about Him. That is the first wonder of it. His friendship crossed all the hoary barriers of sex, and caste, and education, and possession

and in a wide and glorious intimacy He sought and found His friends everywhere, among the learned and the unlearned, the high and the low, the rich and the poor. And the true aristocracy in that day, had it only been recognized, like the true aristocracy in our own day, did we only know it, are those who live in the intimacy of the Prince's presence and who have the rare and radiant distinction to be called His friends.

Let us think a little while upon some of the characteristics of this great friendship; upon some of the distinctive signs of the friends of the Lord. First of all, then, this friendship is characterized by openness of disposition. Some lives are close and closed, and they appear to be almost incapable of friendship. You can never get beyond their doorstep. Their doors are shut, their windows are closed, their blinds are drawn. However long you know them they never let you know anything. Other lives are open to your approach, they open as a flower opens to the gentle siege of the sunshine. These are the people who are capable of friendship. One door after another opens out in the treasury of their soul. You are taken first into the realm of thought, then into the realm of desire and feeling, and then into the innermost room of prayer and praise. Concerning such a soul we say, "I know him through and through." And so it is with the friends of Christ. There is perfect openness between the soul and the Lord. There is openness on the side of the Master. He hides nothing we need to know. "I have set before thee an open door." All things that I have heard of My Father I have made known unto you." "He shall take of Mine and show it unto you." And there must be a similar openness on the side of man. "If any man open the door I will come in and sup with him." There must be no reserve, no sheltered secrets, no private chamber where questionable purpose is hid. The Lord must have the run of the house. He must know all. There must be perfect openness of disposition.

And, secondly, this friendship is distinguished by a responsive sympathy. There must not only be open doors between two friends, there must be sympathetic fellowship. It was asked by a prophet long ago concerning man and his God, "Can two walk together except they be agreed?" If two people walk together they must agree at any rate on two things; they must have a common aim, and they must have a common pace. And the friends of Christ who seek to walk with Him must share His aim, His ends, His goals. They must also keep step with Him and not move either before or behind. We mar the friendship by precipitate haste, and we bruise it by destructive delay. And therefore I say that this high friendship demands a sensitive and responsive sympathy. There must be fellowship in aversions, there must be fellowship in attachments. There must be the same loves and the same hatreds. There must be the same fundamental moral tastes. We must agree on what is bitter, and we must agree on what is sweet. Friendship with the Lord aspires after that wonderful communion which the Master Himself described when He said, "I and My Father are one."

And in the third place this friendship is marked by natural and unreckoned sacrifices. Friendship is never really noble and matured until on both sides it becomes unconsciously sacrificial. Friend must bleed for friend and not see the blood. There are three or four grades of friendship, beginning on an elementary scale which scarcely deserves the name of friendship at all, and rising into a glory of self-abandonment which makes us kinsmen of the

Christ. On the lowest stage there is a friendship which only covets personal gain. It is there for what it can make out of you. On this plane friendship is only association. Love has not yet dawned, for the inmost heart and life of love is an impartation of self. On the second grade there is a friendship which gives, and which likes to display its gift. It loves to stand back and admiringly contemplate its own offerings. It is always conscious when it is giving, how it is giving, and the nature and price of its gifts. It is calculating and not spontaneous. It is never unknowingly generous, it is never unrememberingly bountiful, it is never gloriously and forgetfully prodigal of its own blood. It is a friendship which gives and which carefully registers the amount of its gifts.

And thirdly there is the friendship that is unmindful of its sacrifices. This is a glorious type which, while it gives, has all the gracious feeling of receiving. In its sacrifices it is far more conscious of income than of expenditure; indeed, the sense of expenditure is almost altogether absent. "I was hungered and ye gave Me meat." "Lord, when--?" That is a lofty and radiant plane of achievement. Can any relationship be more intimate and gracious than for two friends to be pouring their life into each other and both of them, unconscious of any sacrifice? And yet perhaps there is even a further height on this glorious tableland of being when, in the unconsciousness of sacrifice, one man hungers for a deeper share in the sufferings of his friend. And that is the craving of the Prince of Glory towards you and me. He hungered and hungers to share our sufferings, to enter into our travail. "He bore our sins and carried our sorrows."

In every pang that rends the heart

The Man of Sorrows has a part.

That must be our craving towards our Saviour-Friend. We must aspire to share His sufferings. It must be our coveted privilege "not only to believe on Him, but also to suffer for His sake." We must enter into "the travail that makes His kingdom come." We must share His sufferings in fighting ignorance, in warring against wrong, and in proclaiming the evangel of love and grace to wayward and indifferent men. This is the high and priceless privilege of the friends of Christ.

And now I have one bit of counsel to offer to those who are seeking to be the friends of the Lord. Keep your friendship with the Lord in good repair. There is a German proverb which says that "Friendship is a plant that we must water often." It must not be allowed to take its chance. Human friendships have to be tended, for there is no fair thing in the world which can thrive in an atmosphere of neglect. And therefore we must carefully attend to our friendship with the Lord. "Friendship should be surrounded with ceremonies and respects." Yes, even the wonderful liberties of friendship are helped by tender courtesies. So is it respecting our friendship with Christ. We must surround it with ceremonies and respects. I believe there is a way of kneeling, a way of going on one's knees, a way of rising from one's knees, which will enrich the intimacy of our freedom with the Lord. "Oh, come, let us worship and bow down."

And as for the Master's side of the friendship, it cannot be put into words. "He is a friend that sticketh closer than a brother." He loves to make friends of the failure, the bruised, the unfortunate, and him that hath no helper. And He wants to befriend thee and me to-day, in all our sins, in all our sorrows, in all our worries, in all the manifold changes of the ever-changing day.

His friendship transforms every road. Every road unveils spiritual wonders when He walks with us, and blessings abound on every side. The very consciousness of His presence begets a peace which is itself the medium of discernment, and we are able, on the most ordinary road, to know some of "the things that God hath prepared for them that love Him."

XX. CONTACT BUT NOT COMMUNION

HERE is a field, and here is the sower sowing the seed. "And some seeds fell by the wayside." And there the seed lies, pregnant with life and fruitfulness, but it cannot get into the ground. The vitalities in the earth and in the seed do not come into fellowship. The miracle of quickening and growing is nearly happening, but it does not happen. A harvest is all but at the birth, but it is not born. So near and yet so far! The seed and the earth touch, but they do not combine. There is contact, but no communion.

And so it is, says the Master, in the field of human life. Great happenings may be exceedingly near and yet appallingly remote. Truth may be up against the soul, and yet there may be no fellowship. The human and the Divine may be in immediate neighbourhood; and there may be no acquaintance. We may brush against God and nothing more. The Divine may be as near the human as the seed to the wayside ground, and still there may be no apprehension. There may be contact, but no communion.

And so this appears to be the character suggested in the Master's words. There is a soul in touch with truth, but not free; in touch with life, but not alive; in touch with God, but not sharing the nature of God. God is near, but the soul does no business. Hands touch, but they do not clasp in holy covenant. There is contact, but no communion.

It is true in the realm of our material environment. God is immediately near in His created world. There is a mystic Immanence which touches us on every side. The desert furze-bush is inhabited by holy flame. Every common place is the home of Deity. "He rideth upon the wings of the wind." "The clouds are His chariots." We may call this poetry, if we please, but we do not banish it from the realm of reality. Men and women of sensitive spirit are aware of a ubiquitous tenant, of an august Presence lighting up the plainest road. God is very near. We are touching Him every moment. But there may be touch and no perception, no fellowship, no inter-passing of relations, no vital correspondence. Tremendous happenings may be near the birth, but nothing is born.

It is equally true in the mystic realms of conscience. The truth in conscience is immediately near to me, as near as the seed that rests upon the wayside. The Divine is in contact with the human. What may we do with it? First, we may not recognize it. It may be a, seed just like many other seeds which have been wafted to us on the wings of the wind. God's saying is mixed up with other sayings. His decree is lost amid the maxims and expediencies of the world. His truth is buried among human guesses and opinions. Or, in the second place, we may give the distinguished Presence in conscience an undistinguished name. We may use some word that will encourage us in lax familiarity and indifference. The Prince of Wales has been given a college name in Oxford, in which all Royal significance is concealed. It is a hail-fellow-well-met name, in which the coming King becomes an ordinary man of the street. Thus may we act with conscience. We may give it a trifling name, and then begin to trifle with it. We may strip it of its imperial purple, and clothe it in a common dress, and then take liberties with it. We may call it a "bogey," and laugh it to scorn. Yes, we may say "bogey," and dismiss it to the delusive shades. Or, thirdly, we may just take the truth into the vital powers of life. We may receive the heavenly Presence and entertain it. We may take the truth into the realm of judgment, to determine our decisions. We may take it into the realm of the will to determine our actions. And so we may fashion the life in the holy likeness of God. What shall we do with the truth? Shall we take it in and assure a harvest, or shall we leave it out and assure a desert The seed touches! Shall it be only contact or communion?

Mark again how the Word of the Lord applies to the secret exercises of worship. When we meet together for public communion God is near, how near we cannot express. We cannot help but touch Him. We are brushing against Him in every moment of the sacred hour. I say we cannot help the contact, but we can refuse the communion. There may be interest but no reverence. There may be graceful postures, but no sterling homage. When we bow to pray there may be touch, but no grip. In the feast of the holy sacrament we may handle the bread, and so touch the very hem of His garment, and yet there may be no sacred union. We may go away from the service in the assumption that we have had communion when we have only been in contact with the Lord. The seed touched the wayside, but it was not taken in.

Once again see how the teaching is illustrated in the realm of common circumstances. The Lord who visited the home at Bethany still comes to the homes of His people. The Lord who worked in the carpenter's shop is still in the centres of labour and business. And the Lord of the evening feast at Emmaus is still a guest at the common meal. In all our customary circumstances the holy Lord is near. We cannot help but touch Him; do we commune with Him? In the sacrament of the common meal, the Lord is with us at the table. "Thou knowest my downsitting and mine uprising." "He was made known unto them in the breaking of bread." He may be so near and yet He may be far away. He may never be counted among the guests. His presence may be ignored. The common meal may be graceless, thankless, Godless, with no enrichment or suggestion of things which are Divine.

And so is it also in the sacrament of common labour. God moves to and fro among our common tasks. He is with us in the gift of bread, and He is with us in the processes by which we earn it. He is lovingly concerned about our daily toil, and He would hearten and enlighten the worker by the strength and comforts of His grace. And yet how truly do we know that the workshop may have nothing of the savour of the temple, and may be regarded as profane. The seed is near, but not in the ground. The Lord is near, but not in the soul. And yet the promise abides: "He shall be with you and shall be in you."

Happily, thrice happily, this alienation can be ended by the exercise of our own choice of will. The very desire to receive the truth draws the seed into the secret place of the soul. The will to commune means that communion has begun. When I kneel in sincerity I am opening the door to the heavenly guest: "If any man will open the door I will come in and sup with him and he with Me." That is the promise of the Master; it has never been re-yoked; it has never been unredeemed. There is no unwillingness on the part of the Lord; the unwillingness rests with us. "If thou wilt!" That is the challenge of the Master; and the willing soul will discover the Lord in the innermost room of the soul.

XXI. THE MORNING BREEZE

IN Walter Pater's "Marius "there is an exquisite description of the impression produced upon him by his first fellowship with a Christian. The Christian was Cornelius, a young noble, a soldier of the Twelfth Legion. "With all the severity of Cornelius there was (at the same time) a breeze of hopefulness--freshness and hopefulness--as of a new morning about him." This delicate phrase, "the breeze of morning," came into my mind as I was reading Paul's letter to Timothy, and the account which the great apostle gives of the helpful ministry of his friend Onesiphorus. The Apostle says, "He oft refreshed me," and the suggestion is that of the coming of a current of fresh air, a reviving coolness after heat. This obscure disciple was like Cornelius who ministered to Marius, and he brought renewal of spirits to the great Apostle of the Gentiles. His was the ministry of the morning breeze.

Now it is a significant thing that the Apostle needed the refreshment. He had his seasons of fainting when the spirit grew distressed. What could there be in his life to hold his soul in gloomy servitude? There is no depression like that which waits upon natures that are intense. The passionate are familiar with depths that are unknown to the temperate. And Paul, with all his burning enthusiasms, had his moments of faintness. For one reason, there was the undying mistrust of the ultra-conservative Jews. They suspected the genuineness of his apostleship. They suspected the orthodoxy of his message. From end to end of his life this vigilant and often malicious mistrust hung around about his soul. And of all things that can come to a messenger of Christ, there is nothing more wearing and wearying than a spirit of mistrust. It chokes you. It smothers you. It makes you faint.

And then, for a second thing, there was the corruption breaking out in the young Churches he had newly planted. To a man with high ideals these rude realities would occasion deep depression. I was with a gardener a little while ago, who was taking me round the garden-beds, and pointing to one little plot where almost every flower seemed touched with blight, he said, "It is very disheartening." And when the Apostle Paul looked over his garden plot at Corinth, and saw how the fair flowers were smitten with moral blight, he became depressed and faint.

And, thirdly, there was the contemplation of his own slow progress in the world of the Spirit. "The prize of the high calling "seemed far away, and like more obscure disciples he would sometimes feel as though the journey were scarce begun. In the seventh chapter to the Romans we have glimpses of the Apostle when this mood was upon him, and when he needed all his reserves to keep going. Well, in these ways and in others, he came to times of depression when his fainting soul was in need of refreshment.

And in these times of fainting God sent His messenger with the morning breeze. Onesiphorus was a bringer of fresh air to the faint. It is beautiful that an obscure disciple could be the minister of refreshment to a great apostle. The ventilator in a room is often an exceedingly plain article, ungainly, when contrasted with more luxurious things around, but it is the medium of refreshment, the channel through which the air travels, that makes life easy and pleasant. And humble people can be the channels of the heavenly birth to greater people who are faint. Every minister knows such folk in his congregation. They are not heavily endowed with treasured attractions. They have neither gifts of culture nor of wealth, but they are makers of atmosphere. They make it easier for other people to breathe.

I wonder what windows Onesiphorus opened to let in the morning air upon the fainting spirit of the Apostle? Perhaps he directed him to some forgotten promise, some word stored with heavenly energy which the great Apostle had forgotten. When Bishop Butler was dying there came a moment of faintness over his soul, and an obscure chaplain who was in the chamber, whose name is not given to us, reminded the Bishop of some dynamic promise of the Master, and his spirit was refreshed. Or, perhaps, Onesiphorus would mention to the Apostle some exploit in his ministry of which he had never heard: "Let me tell you what happened at Ephesus after you had gone away. Let me tell you what happened to so-and-so after he had listened to your message about the heavenly love." And Paul would listen and listen until the faintness gave place to hope and quiet trust. Or, perhaps, again Onesiphorus would retrace the pathway of the Apostle's life, and point out to him unremembered mercies which were scattered like flowers along the road; or he would show him how past difficulties had been surmounted by the powers of grace, or how other seasons of depression had been fruitful because the barren desert was in reality a garden of God. Or, once again Onesiphorus might dip into his own history and bring forth testimonies to the triumphant power of Eternal Love. He would diffidently bring forth his own witnesses, and the story would be as morning air to him who was sick and faint.

Well, now, this kind of service is the one that is most needed in the Church of Christ. We want people who carry atmosphere and are ministers of refreshment. And such people will instinctively go where the ministry is most required. It is a beautiful lineament in the character of Onesiphorus which is given in the Apostle's phrase, "He was not ashamed of my chain." The great scholar, and convert, and saint, and apostle was held in servitude, but we know what a name he gave to his chain. He called it "my bonds in Christ." He linked his very servitude to the Lord. He took his restrictions, his limitations, his impediments, and surveyed them in their association with the Christ. But a man's chain often lessens the circle of his friends. The chain of poverty keeps many people away, and so does the chain of unpopularity. When a man is in high repute he has many friends. When he begins to wear a chain the friends are apt to fall away. But the ministers of the morning breeze love to come to the shades of night. They delight to minister in the region of despondency, and where the bonds lie heaviest upon the soul. "He was not ashamed of my chain." The chain was really an allurement. It gave speed to his feet and urgency to his ministry.

And is not this the very friendship of the Lord Jesus? He is not ashamed of our chains. When He was with us in the flesh He amazed people by His familiarity with the victims who were held in bonds. "He is gone to be guest with a man that is a sinner." He was not ashamed of his chain. "He eateth and drinketh with publicans and sinners." Their chains did not repel Him. "He remembereth us in our low estate." He brings the ministry of refreshment to those who languish in prison. "He is the Lord of the morning to the children of the night."

XXII. NO BREATH

"THERE was no breath in them." There was everything except breath. They were perfectly articulated bodies, but they were devoid of inspiration. The organized bones were as impotent as when they lay scattered over the desolate fields, organization had accomplished nothing. The lack was vital. There was an absence of life.

And this, says the prophet, is the symbol of a common tragedy in the lives of men and nations. Movements stop just short of inspiration. Fine organizations have no soul. There is "noise" and there is "shaking," but there is no quickening wind from God. There is combination, but no communion. Bone comes to bone, and there are sinews and skin, but there is no air, no enlivening power from the heart of God.

We may find an illustration of the prophet's symbol in the domain of words. A dictionary is a valley of dry bones. It is a mass of dismembered words scattered like dislocated bones, every word isolated from every other word, lying there bleached and dry. Well, a man thinks himself to be a poet, and he comes to the dictionary, and he begins to gather the words together "bone to his bone." He joins them in the friendliest concord. He organizes them in metrical rhymes. Every law of grammar and metre and melody is honoured. The association is sweet and soft and orderly and--dead! It is a beautiful corpse, but there is no breath in it; it jingles, but it is not poetry.

Or we may go to the verbal valley of dry bones, and we may gather the scattered members together and construct a prayer, fitting bone to bone, giving it sinews and covering it with flesh and skin. And there it is, a decent orderly thing, but dead! We say our prayers, but we do not pray. We marshal our words, but we do not aspire. We present a corpse instead of a breathing. And here is a poor publican, with a meagre little handful of words, which he sobs out rather than repeats: "Lord, be merciful to me a sinner," and "the words stand up an exceeding great army," and they take the kingdom of heaven by storm.

Sometimes we go to the dictionary, the valley of dry bones, and we gather its words together to construct a creed. The articles of the creed are most carefully shaped and fitted together with exquisite association. Word is joined to word in precise succession, and sentence linked with sentence in exact logical agreement. It is strengthened with the sinews of philosophy, and furnished with the flesh and skin of tender emotion, and there it is, an organized statement of belief! And we may repeat it with the semblance of life. There may be a "noise" and the "shaking," but no inspiration, no aspiration, no lowly confession of trust or prayer; and the mystic unseen ministers, who watch the souls of things, proclaim the heavenly judgment, "there is no breath in them." Another man gropes for a little handful of words, and fits them uncertainly together, and stammers them out before the Lord: "Lord, I believe, help Thou mine unbelief." And the Kingdom is taken.

In the Church that bears the name of Christ we may have everything but the essential thing. We may have order and decency and reverence, and the appearance of fraternity. Bone may come to bone, and there may be the sinews and even the flesh and skin, and yet there may be no pervading breath, no mysterious and unifying life. We may have a congregation, but not a communion; we may have an assembly, but not an army; we may have a fellowship roll, but not of those who are counted alive, and whose names "are written in the Lamb's Book of Life." We may be just a crowd, and not "the family of the living God."

We may have prayers, but no prayer. We may have petitions, but no real intercession. We may have posture and homage, but no supplication. We may have exquisite ritual, but no holy worship. We may have what men call "a finished service," and yet there may be nothing of the violence of a vital faith. We may have benevolences, but no sacrifice. We may have the appearance of service, but no shedding of blood. The Church may be only an organized corpse.

But when the breath comes, how then? The breath of God converts an organization into an organism, it transforms a combination into a fellowship, a congregation into a church, a mob into an army. That breath came into a little disciple-band, a band that was worm-eaten by envy and jealousy, and weakened by timidity and fear, and it changed it into a spiritual army that could not be checked or hindered by "the world, the flesh, and the devil." And when the same breath of God comes into a man of "parts," a man of many faculties and talents, sharpened by culture, drilled and organized by discipline, it endows him with the veritable power of an army and makes him irresistible. "And Peter filled with the holy breath!" How can we compute the value and the significance and the power of that unifying association? Peter himself becomes an army, "an army of the living God." If the Church were filled with men of such glorious spiritual endowment, what would be the tale of exploits, what new chapters would be added to the Acts of the Apostles?

XXIII. BLINDING THE MIND

THERE is a phrase of the Apostle Paul which contains a warning peculiarly relevant to the times through which we are passing. It is this: "The god of this world hath blinded the minds." What is the significance of the phrase, "The god of this world"? Here is a certain evil influence personified. A certain immoral energy or contagion is conceived and presented as an active, aggressive, personal force, which deliberately seeks to dwarf, and bruise, and lame the richly-dowered souls of men. He is elsewhere depicted as of princely line, with imposing retinues and armies, moving stealthily amid human affairs, and inciting men to rebellion against the holy sovereignty of God. He is represented as "the prince of the powers of the air," subtle and persuasive as an atmosphere, insinuating himself into the most sacred privacies and invading even the most holy place. He is "the god of this world," receiving homage and worship, the god to whom countless thousands offer ceaseless sacrifice, while the holy Lord of grace and glory is neglected or defied. I am not now concerned with this personification, whether it be literalistic or merely figurative; but I am concerned with the reality of the power itself, whose seductive energy corrupts our holiest treasures, and blunts and spoils the finest perceptions of the soul.

Now, everybody is familiar with the characteristics of this destructive ministry. There is no need of abstruse or hair-splitting analysis. The issues are obtrusive; we have only to examine our own souls and their besetments, and the peril is revealed. We may have dropped the personification, but we recognize the energy which is personified. We may have abandoned the figure, but we are familiar with the thing. We may no longer speak of "the god of this world," but "worldliness" itself is palpable and rampant. This is our modern phraseology. We speak of "the worldly" and "the unworldly," but unfortunately the terms are very loosely and indefinitely used, or used with a quite perverse significance. The "unworldly "is too often identified with the "other-worldly," and is interpreted as an austere isolation from all festivity, and from the hard, hand-soiling concerns of practical life. And on the other hand, "worldliness" is too often identified with gaiety, or levity, or prodigality, with drink and pride, with theatrical glamour and vulgar sheen. But these interpretations do not touch the heart of the matter. What, then, is worldliness? Worldliness is life without ideals, life without moral vistas, life devoid of poetic vision. It is life without the halo, life without the mystic nimbus which invests it with venerable and awful sanctity. It is imprisonment within the material, no windows opening out upon ethereal, moral, or altruistic ends. It is the five senses without the moral sense. It is quickness to appetite and dulness to conscience. It is engrossment in sensations, it is heedlessness to God's "awful rose of dawn." It is rank materialism.

Now this powerful contagion operates in the deprivation of sight. Materialism and moral blindness stand in the relation of cause and effect. "The god of this world hath blinded the minds." That is to say, a practical materialism destroys the eyes of the soul. The materialistic life deadens the conscience, and in the long run puts it to death. The materialistic life stupefies the imagination, and in the long run makes it inoperative. The materialistic life defiles the affections, and converts their crystalline lens into a minister of darkness and night. The materialistic life coarsens the spiritual instincts, and renders them non-appreciative of things unseen. And so it is with all the vision-powers of life; a practical materialism plugs or scales them and makes the spirit blind.

But I will still further narrow the interpretation, and confine this article to that aspect of worldliness which is concerned with the bare pursuit of material gain. If "the god of this world" must be given a single name, let the name be Mammon, and let the love of money be the worship which is offered at his shrine. And does the god of money blind the mind? Let it get into the pulpit, and everybody knows the result. The spiritual heavens become opaque, and there is no awe-inspiring discernment of "things unseen." Everybody recognizes its destructiveness in the ministry, but everybody does not equally recognize the destructiveness in other lives and other professions. But the moral issues are one and the same; always and everywhere the god of money blinds the mind.

Let me give a Scriptural illustration of its nefarious work. A woman, who had been spiritually enfranchised by the Lord, and who had been led out of the dreary, wan land of sin into the fair, bright lily-land of God's eternal peace, brought an alabaster box of ointment, very precious, and anointed her Deliverer's feet. And there was one standing by, who looked upon it with uninspired and unillumined eyes, and said, "To what purpose is this waste?" . . . "This he said . . . because he was a thief, and carried the bag!" He was the victim of the god of money, and he was blind, and he could see no beauty or grace in this passionate love-offering of an, emancipated child of God. There was nothing winsome about the woman that he should commend her; and, more than that, when he looked upon the woman's Lord there was "no beauty" that he should desire Him! "What will ye give me, and I will deliver Him unto you? And they covenanted with him for thirty pieces of silver." And for that "thirty pieces of silver" he sold his Lord! May we not add, "the god of this world" had blinded his mind?

But there is no. need for us to go back to those remote days for illustration of the truth. Every succeeding century has abounded in confirmation of its truth. But let me confine myself to witnesses from modern history. I know of no more shameful page in the history of our country than the page which tells the story of our early demeanour in the American Civil War. The North was valorously intent upon lifting the tyranny of the South, and letting the bond-slave free. And vast multitudes of our people sympathized with the callous and slave-holding South, and ranged themselves in bitter antagonism to the chivalrous North. And what was the explanation? Just this, they were unable to see the interests of humanity because of their interests in cotton. They couldn't see the slave for the dollar, or they saw him only as a chattel to be despised. Henry Ward Beecher came over to expostulate with our countrymen, and to seek to open their eyes. He came here to plead for the slaves--those slaves unveiled to us in the bleeding pages of "Uncle Tom's Cabin." He came to Liverpool. Now listen to a contemporary document and you will think you are reading the Press of the past few weeks. "It would be impossible for tongue or pen adequately to describe the scenes at the meeting. The great hall was packed to the crushing point. The mob was out in force. The interruptions were incessant: cat-calls, groans, and hisses." And at what part of the meeting did the disorder culminate? It was when Beecher, bit by bit, got out these sentences and rammed them home: "When I was twelve years old, my father hired Charles Smith, a man as black as lamp-black, to work on his farm. I slept with him in the same room. (Oh! oh!) Ah, that don't suit you. (Uproar.) I ate with him at the same table; I sang with him out of the same hymn-book; I cried when he prayed over me at night; and if I had serious impressions of religion early in life, they were due to the fidelity and example of that poor, humble farm-labourer, black Charles Smith. (Tremendous uproar.)" What think you of the significance of that uproar? They saw no moral dignity in Charles Smith that they should desire him. That Liverpool mob could not see the slave because they were so intent upon the dollar.

Read the chivalrous history of the good Lord Shaftesbury. In his early manhood, when he began his noble crusade of emancipation, women and girls were employed in coal-mines, as beasts of burden. Their condition haunted him, and became a nightmare which possessed him day and night, and he set about to ameliorate their lot. He sought to prohibit their employment. With what result? The mine-owners were up and in arms. "It spells ruin to our trade!" They could not see the degradation for the gold. They feared a shrinking purse more than a shrunken womanhood. They could not see the woman for the bank. But Lord Ashley disregarded their cries, and at length he had the supreme happiness of putting a stop to this infamous sort of labour by an act which declared that, after a certain limited period, no woman or girl should ever again be employed in our collieries and mines.

When Queen Victoria came to the throne, a dispute with China was developing into a very ugly menace. Soon after it broke out into open war. And what did we fight about? We fought for the right of Great Britain to force a destructive trade upon a people who did not want it, in spite of the protestations of its government, and in spite of all such national opinion as could find a public expression. There was money in it for Britain, there was revenue in it for India, and therefore China had got to have it! It is China's burden, China's curse, China's appalling woe, and still we force it on her. And the explanation is clear. We cannot see the evil for the revenue. We cannot see the wasting victim for the swelling exchequer. Some day Britain will get the gold-dust out of her eyes, and then she will see--she will see the reeking opium dens, and the emaciated manhood, and the devastated families, and the blighted race, and in her shame she will wash her hands of the traffic, and decree the emancipation of a people. At present, money plugs the eyes.

And there is very great need that in our own day we deliver ourselves from the servitude of this mammon. In our day, when the Spirit of God is at work in our midst, inciting dissatisfaction and unrest, and creating a ferment among the peoples, our vision and our sympathy can be dulled and checked by the common love of money. The peril is insidious, and it invades even the most holy place. The spirit of greed dwells not alone among the wealthy and the well-to-do, it can make its home with people of slender means. What we need, above all things, is to have our eyes anointed with the eye-salve of grace, that so our vision may be single and simple, and we may have the mind of Christ. What we need is unscaled sight, and with unscaled sight there will come fresh and healthy sympathies, and an eager participation in every chivalrous crusade.

XXIV. THE SOUL IN THE MARKET

I USE these words, "The Soul in the Market," to characterize the second temptation of our Lord. Here is a soul face to face with the supreme enemy of souls. The enemy of souls creates in life the atmosphere of the market. He proposes a transaction in the nature of an exchange. He suggests a bargain and makes an offer. What are the terms? What does he offer? "The kingdoms of the world and the glory of them." What does he ask in return? The worship and service of the soul. "If Thou wilt fall down and worship me." That is to say, he offers a temporality and demands a spirituality. He offers a reputation and demands a character. He offers a great "spread," but insists upon a stooping soul. He offers a show of liberty, but his terms are spiritual servitude. He offers possessions, but the price is degradation. He proposes a profitable exchange, and for the treasures of the soul he offers the treasures of the world. Make him supreme monarch in the empire of the soul, and he will make us kings in material domains. That is the essential bargain. The soul is in the market in Vanity Fair.

Let us inspect the character of the temptation a little more closely. The air was filled with the rumour of a coming king and of the restoration of kingdoms. Everywhere was the sense of thrill and expectancy. Men's eyes were scouring the horizon for one that should come. And now excitement was intensified, for there had appeared by the Jordan a desert prophet with the old authoritative word and mien, proclaiming the news of the King's coming, and the Kingdom of God was at hand. The King had left His palace! He was on the road! "Prepare ye the way of the Lord."

And what did they expect to see? They looked for a king who should be clothed in the mysteries of unshared powers, before whom the kingdoms of the world would lie prostrate in awed and affrighted obeisance. He was to be a sort of Prospero, with invisible Ariels at his command, going forth on his decrees to charm or to paralyze, to bind or to free. The coming king would set up the throne of his glory in Jerusalem, the place of his presence would make the grandeur of empires sombre; he would have his feet upon the neck of kings, and he would lay their valiant ones in the dust. "Then cometh Jesus, and the devil taketh Him into an exceeding high mountain, and showed Him all the kingdoms of the world, and the glory of them, and said unto Him, All these things will I give Thee, if Thou wilt fall down and worship me.'"

Let us mark the subtlety of the snare. Think how much the young Nazarene might accomplish by the possession of a carnal rule. He could ride abroad redressing human wrongs. He could strike the weapon from the hand of the oppressor. He could destroy the tyranny of iniquitous taxation. He could lighten the burden of the poor. The sovereignty of kingdoms would give Him the ministry of freedom, and wherever men were in servitude, He could lead them into glorious liberty. "All these things will I give Thee!" What are the terms of the exchange? "If Thou wilt fall down and worship me." The devil is seeking his exchanges in the region of the soul. He is seeking them in the realm of spiritual homage and posture, in the secret place of worship and ideal. "Alter thy soul posture. Readjust thy secret homage. Change thy spiritual inclinations. Dilute the stringency of thy holiness. Change thy heavenly principles for loose expediencies. Change thy impossible ideals for working compromises. Change thy clear, straight sight for winks and nods and wiles. Change thy serene wisdom for sharp subtlety. Change thy unvarnished truth for the oil of flattery. Make more of appearances. Let life be more a game, a scheme, an artifice, and less of an exalted crusade. "All these things I will give thee, if thou wilt only play my game. Thou shalt appoint the goal, but mine shall be the way to reach it. Thine shall be the end, but mine shall be the means." Such were the terms of the proposed exchange.

And the answer? The Master's answer came sharp, immediate, peremptory, and absolute: "Get thee behind Me, Satan!" Our Master would not change the inclination of His soul by the shadow of a turning. He would not deflect His steps by a hair's breadth from the path of holiness and truth. To gain kingdoms and the glory of them He would not haul down the holy flag waving on the citadel of His soul. He would not worship in the house of Rimmon. He would not wipe out the Ten Commandments and write ten corn-promises in their place. He would not exchange the fair, clear, sunny ideals of the Divine hills for the will-o'-the-wisps of "the world and the flesh and the devil." "Get thee behind Me, Satan, for it is written thou shalt worship the Lord thy God, and Him only shalt thou serve."

Let no one imagine that with the defeat of this temptation the same temptation never returned. If I interpret the Master's life aright, the temptation returned again and again, with precisely the same enticements, always changing its attire, but always with the same motive, and armed with the same destructive quest. The Lord was always being tempted to use illicit means in the interests of the heavenly kingdom, to take forbidden ways to apparently legitimate ends. We have an instance of the return of the temptation when He was enticed by His own brethren to worship at the loud, garish altar of egotism and self-display. "If Thou do these things, show Thyself to the world." Copy the ways of the world and make a noise! Advertise Thyself! He would have none of it. "He shall not strive nor cry, neither shall any man hear His voice in the street."

There is a further example of the return when Simon Peter sought to entice his Lord to take the easy road and to seek His throne by the flowery path of comfort. "Then Peter took Him and began to rebuke Him, saying, This shall not be unto Thee.'" And the Lord again answered with the sharp response He made to the first temptation, "Get thee behind Me, Satan." Christ would have no illicit compromises. He would make no bargains with indolence. He would offer no incense at the altar of worldly wisdom. "He set His face steadfastly to go to Jerusalem," and He walked the thorny, flinty road to Calvary and the Cross, and this was His one response to all alluring besetments by the way: "Thou shalt worship the Lord thy God, and Him only shalt thou serve."

XXV. TERMINUS AND THOROUGHFARE

ONE of the most deadly temptations in life is to mistake a thoroughfare for a terminus, and to regard what is intended to be a means as an ultimate end. When we make a material thing a terminus we only exist; when we make the material a thoroughfare to the spiritual we begin to live. And, therefore, one of the determining questions in life, where subtle snares abound, is this: Shall the material be a terminus or a thoroughfare, a goal or a passage, a means or an end? Shall we seek to live "by bread alone," or, using bread as a subordinate means, shall we find our true life in the unseen? And here is the Saviour's answer. We live not in material things or in material quests, but in Divine relations. "This is life, to know Thee." By "bread alone" the body can exist; man needs the bread of the world; he can only live by the hidden manna of Divine communion.

Consider the reach of this principle in the light of one or two of its multitudinous applications. Apply the principle to nature, to our association with the wonders of the natural world. Our temptation is to dwell on the material side of nature, and never apprehend the spiritual significance of the Divine world. We stop at "bread"; we do not push through to God. There is a type of man to whom nature makes no sort of refined appeal. He seems to be insensible to its presence. His powers are held in a kind of benumbment. There is a second type of man who discovers in nature higher ministries of physical inspiration and delight. His senses are gratified. He is charmed by the play of colour, he is fascinated by the minstrelsy of song, he is exhilarated by the delicacies of flavour and perfume. There is a third type of man who rises to an aesthetic appreciation of nature. He exercises artistic and poetic discernment. Imagination is now at work, and delicate fancy, and a world of romance is unveiled. Idylls are born and lyrics are sung. But there is a fourth type of man who has a spiritual apprehension of nature, who holds communion with its spiritual world, who uses it as a thoroughfare to the Divine, who

116

passes by its "bread," giving thanks for the bread, to find the true significance in God. He moves with awed and wondering soul through "the light of setting suns" to "the light that never was on sea or land," and through the apocalypse of the changing clouds to "the rainbow round about the throne." The outer bread conducts him to the hidden manna, and behind the world of the senses he discovers the world invisible, incorruptible, and full of glory.

Let us further apply the principle to our conception of history. It is possible to approach history and to abide in its outer courts it is possible to go further, and in history to find "the Word of God." We may have a materialistic conception of history, and when we survey its crowded procession we may see only the contention of material forces, and in its changing triumphs we may see only the changing ascendency of the brute. We may have a spiritual conception of history, and behind all its perspiring tumults and noise and armies and brutal riot and disorder we may discern a spiritual presence and hear a ghostly word, the word "proceeding from the mouth of God." In my own schooldays the learning of history was the memorizing of bald and innutritious dates, or we were ceaselessly watching the glamour and pageantry of kings and queens, or we were following the doings of armies and gazing upon rivers of blood. Since those days our attitude towards history has changed. We are not so much concerned with the fittings of monarchs as with the movements of peoples, not with the life of the palace but with happenings in the cottage, not with the growth of armies but with the growth of freedom.

But even with this revived attitude we are still outside the temple, and may still be tempted to abide in its material and social passages, and not press through to God. What is God saying in history? What is "the word proceeding from the mouth of God"? What is He saying in the history of the empires of the ancient world? What is the speech of events? What is the clearly defined word of results and destiny? In this way we are to press through the garish shows of things, past the sheen and the pain and the blood, and we are to listen to the eternal word of the living God.

But the principle may not only be applied to the history of nations but to the record of the individual life. What is the Divine word in my own past life? Let me get through to that. I shall be tempted to take an unspiritual view of my own past. I shall be inclined to fix upon its cleverness, or its want of cleverness, or its fortune, or its misfortune, its luck, or its chance. I shall be foolish to stop there. It is the way of wisdom to push through the material, the outer furniture and equipment and to get into the secret room and hear "the word proceeding from the mouth of God." What does He say to us through our yesterdays? "He that hath ears to hear let him hear."

So have I tried to show how the principle may be applied to nature and to history. It might be similarly applied to ordinary duty, to its outer halls and its inspired secrets; to common work, its outer form and its spiritual significance. Indeed, the principle has range of application to all the manifold relations and interests of human life. Everywhere we are tempted to make a terminus of what was intended to be a thoroughfare, to stop at "bread," and not get through to God. We are snared to stop at the material, the formal, the ritualistic, the symbolic, and we thereby miss the life indeed, and the heavenly bread that alone sustains it. We are enticed to remain in the outer halls of being, and we miss the secret room where is set the appointed feast.

The snare is about us when we meet for worship. We meet as immortal souls. The enemy of souls is present to entice the immortal to be satisfied with the material, the formal, the musical, the sensational, with the rites and rubrics of worship, and to have no concern for a personal communion with God. He seeks to make us contented with forms and postures, to make the hymn and the anthem and the sermon a terminus and not a highway by which we find "the secret place of the Most High." It is our daily wisdom to have the snare in mind, and to reject all enticements that keep us from our rightful inheritance in the heavenly places in Christ Jesus.

XXVI. THE DESTRUCTION AT NOONTIDE

THERE is a peril in the garish day. There are destructive things that are only bred in the long-continued splendour. They awake and prowl about in the noon. In the deep shadows of the. deeper night they sleep in impotence. "It is the bright day that brings forth the adder." A. summer of unbroken sunshine is not the invincible guardian of the public health. It favours some forms of disease. It may generate a lassitude which gives disease its chance. The glare may become the ally of infirmity.

And now I can see the significance of the psalmist's words, "the destruction that wasteth at noonday." A secret consumption may make its home in the realm of the sunbeam. Our radiant successes may house our most awful foes. Our prosperity may be like some sun-drenched realm in the tropics-- the hunting-ground of the plague. It may be we were safer in the grey, chill twilight of precariousness and uncertainty than we are in the steady brightness of a cloudless noon. We were, perhaps, more secure when a little fear was in our life than we are when the last shadow of care has melted away.

Now what perils are these which hide themselves in the brightness of noon? What enemies emerge in our prosperity? I think that one of the first perils of the noontide is the eclipse of the spiritual relations of life. The sunniest days are not the best for the discernment of far distances. There is a haze in the fierce light that veils the remote horizon. And when our life attains to its burning noon we are apt to lose the land that is very far off. The large relationships of things are eclipsed. Our eyes are lured from the further issues, life's ultimate goals. We become the prisoners of the immediate hour. The things of sense hem us round about, and the transient becomes our all. It is amazingly difficult to keep sight and hold of the eternal when the immediate hour is so brilliant. The very pomp of success seems big enough to satisfy, and we do not want the long vision of the things that endure. And thus we lose them. And yet we are so mesmerized by the present glare that we are not conscious of the loss. I have seen a child so fascinated by a glittering toy that its mother could leave the room and never be missed. That is a subtle peril of life's brilliant noon. We may become so absorbed as not to miss the God we have lost. The glitter of gold can make us forget the glory of God. Some earthly prize dazzles us, and "the prize of the high calling of God in Christ Jesus" is blurred. And all this is "the destruction that wasteth at noonday."

Another great peril of our noontide is a narrowing of the sympathies. In the fierce glare of summer the rivers shrink in their beds. And in the sunny season of triumph and prosperity the streams of our sympathy are apt to grow scanty as in a time of drought. Cloudy, rainy days refresh the springs. Sorrows keep the emotions moist and fluent. Defeat makes us very sympathetic. The obituary columns have a new significance when our own family has written a record there. We look at a cripple with new eyes when one of our own is lame. But when no clouds have passed across our sky we are very prone to lose communion with the children of night. At any rate, that is our peril. When we are prosperous we become encased with pride, and pride is a non-conductor, and the vibrations that beat upon us from the gloomy house of sorrow are never perceived. We can become "past feeling," and lose our correspondence with our fellow-men. The noonday may be a minister of alienation between man and man.

And a third peril of the noonday is what George Adam Smith calls "the atheism of force." The successful man is prone to magnify might without reference to right; carnal power becomes the treasure to be desired. Success is life's end, and success is its own justification. Be like a cow! Trample down a thousand wild flowers and river grasses to get your drink, but get your drink! To get on is the aim. Never mind about getting up! And so life loses its ideals, its dignities, its elevations. It loses the vertical and becomes merely horizontal. It has ambitions, but no aspirations. It has push, but no worship. It has belief in expediencies, but it loses its belief in

God. Instead of "worshipping the Lord, thy God, with all thy strength," it worships the strength of self. And this is one of the subtlest perils of the noonday of success. In our pride we raise our altar to our own right arm. "By the strength of our own hand we have done it."

There is only one security from these perils. It is "the secret place of the Most High." In that secret Presence we dwell under the cooling shadow of the Almighty! There will be no haze with our heat. No earth-born cloud will veil the Supreme. Our great God will be to us as "the shadow of a great rock," and we shall not be dizzied in the burning noon of our prosperity and triumph. We can be successful and yet be safe, but the secret is with God. "He shall not fear men when heat cometh." "The arrow that flieth by day" shall never reach his soul. In the noonday he shall be immune, for "the mouth of the Lord hath spoken it."

The strength of God's grace has been triumphantly manifest in men and women who have spent years in the sunshine. Prosperity has beamed upon them, but they have remained unspoiled. Success after success has poured its radiance around them, but the graces of their spirit do not fade. Some protective air seems to wrap them round about, a defence against the fierceness of the favouring beams. They are defended by the ministries of the Holy Spirit. They can have ease and not be wasted. They can even be wealthy and yet be in the kingdom of humility and peace. They can "pass through the fire and not be burned," for in the fire there is One with them "like unto the Son of Man," and they walk unscathed.

XXVII. THE BENEDICTION OF THE SNOW

THE student of the Word of God, and, indeed, the student of human life, is greatly impressed with the amazing variety of the Divine processes in the culture of the soul. "As the rain cometh down and the snow from heaven and watereth the earth and maketh it bring forth and bud. . . ." These two ministries, so strangely contrasted--the rain and the snow--are equally the friends of the bountiful harvest. That rain should be linked with the harvest I can quite well understand; but one is startled with the range of the vision which connects the snow with the ripened seed. It is reasonable that the delicate dew should be related to the delicate bud, but it is a larger outlook that connects the frosty night with the opening leaf. It is a congenial thought which links the wooing zephyr with the yellowing grain. But here the kinship is made with the cutting blast. Here we are shown the relation of ice to the waving corn! It is this breadth of the process, comprehending such startling contraries, that makes one see the variety of the discipline in the Divine culture of the individual and the race.

The rain provides a most beautiful figure of the softening ministries of grace. It is a fitting expression of the tender mercies of our God. The rain is typical of all the gentle, genial providences, the April weather of mingled sunshine and shower. We have all known these seasons, for we have all experienced them, the seasons when God's love has played upon us like rain upon the hard ground, and when "the barren ground has become a pool and the thirsty land springs of water." No Christian disciple has walked along with the Master, and especially in times of sore affliction, without the knowledge of that gentle consolation when God "comes down like rain upon the mown grass."

But the snow, too, is in the process of Divine culture. There is a place for the frost, the chill, and the winter. The snow is an apparent foe to the purposed bud and seed. It is repressive rather than expressive. It seems to be the minister of death rather than of life, hastening decay rather than promoting growth. And yet the snow is the servant of the harvest. It "cometh down from heaven," it "maketh the earth to bring forth and bud." And thus it is that the cold, cutting discipline in life, for which the snow provides the symbol, is also a servant of the spiritual harvest, and generates and nourishes the flowers and fruits of the perfected life.

Sometimes we can see quite clearly how the harvest of the soul has been helped by the frost and the snow. Winter possesses a life. The grey days come and the cold, dark nights. And then some grace appears, some fine reverence, some chaste reserve, some beautiful modesty, some violet of the spirit, like crocus or gentian revealing itself under the melting coverlet of Alpine snows. It was not there before the snow had fallen, but now it lifts its lowly head before the face of an approving heaven. Let me quote one or two examples of spiritual graces and purposes which have been gendered and nourished beneath the snow robe. Here is one: "Before I was afflicted I went astray, but now I have kept Thy word." Something was born in the severities of affliction; the virtue of fidelity was nourished in the wintry day. And here is another: "It is good for me that I have been afflicted, that I might learn Thy statutes." Here is a faculty that is strengthened by the frost. Affliction adds to the man's worth. The grace of refined perception was found in the day of the falling snow. There is a third suggestive example in the life of Hezekiah: "In those days was Hezekiah sick unto death." The gloom of affliction settled upon his soul; the snow was falling! Now, if we turn to the day when the winter is over, we shall find "flowers appear on the earth." Listen to this word when Hezekiah was recovered of his sickness: "I shall go softly all my years." The snow brought the flowers of delicacy and gentleness and considerateness, and never again would he break the bruised reed.

And here is the Apostle Paul, full of love, full of ardour, burning with passionate quest in the service of his Lord. He was an Apostle of the Kingdom, and through his ministry the evangel of grace was being carried from city to city, from land to land, from clime to clime. He was a glorious sower of the heavenly seed, and there was promise of rich and bountiful harvest. And then the snow began to fall. Cruel, biting blasts blew about his ministry. The evangel appeared to be icebound, and the evangelist himself was held in servitude in Rome. Now turn to the record, to the words written while the snow was yet falling: "The things that happened unto me have turned out rather unto the furtherance of the Gospel." Again we have a harvest helped by the wintry day. Expansion is gained from the agent of apparent restriction. The frost is the nurse of multiplying growth.

Let me give one other example taken from the more general fields of literature. I find it in that great passage in Shakespeare where Cardinal Wolsey is passing out of the glory and pomp of carnal grandeur into the cold wintry gloom of isolation and neglect.

Farewell, a long farewell, to all my greatness!
This is the state of man: to-day he puts forth
The tender leaves of hope; to-morrow blossoms,
And bears his blushing honours thick upon him;
The third day comes a frost, a killing frost,
And--when he thinks, good easy man, full surely
His greatness is a-ripening--nips his root,
And then he falls, as I do.

The frost has come, the snow is falling! But is that the end, a blighted, stricken, withered life? Let us read again: "I feel my heart new open'd." The frost is the minister of the opening, the snow is the servant of a quickened life. Let me read once more:

Cromwell: How does your grace?

Wolsey: Why, well;

Never so truly happy, my good Cromwell. I know myself now; and I feel within me A peace above all earthly dignities, A still and quiet conscience.

And so I say the snow is the minister in the development of the Lord's design. If we had no snow in our lives there would be no chivalry, no springs of tenderness, no brimming rivers of noble compassion. If there were no snow I am afraid there might be no violets, and life would not attain those holy graces which shone in the life of the Son of God. "He learned obedience by the things that he suffered." If the soul had no winter it might miss its intimate vision of God.

XXVIII. NEEDLESS REGRETS!

"IF Thou hadst been here my brother had not died." That is a Scriptural example of a very familiar experience. It illustrates a most commonplace form of grief. It is an example of needless regrets. "If Thou hadst been here my brother had not died." If we had arranged things a little differently, how different might have been the issues! If we had taken another turning, what a contrast in our destiny! If only we had done so-and-so, Lazarus might have been with us still! My readers will recognize the familiarity of the utterance. It is the expression of a common human infirmity. Its sound travels through the years like the haunting sigh of a low moan. "If only . . . !" "If only . . . !" And the pathetic cry is with us to-day. It is usually born on the morning after a crisis, and it sometimes continues until the plaintive soul itself goes home to rest. It is a sorrow that consumes like a gangrene. It drains away the vital strength. If by some gracious ministry it could be ended, and the moan changed into trustful quietude, an enormous load would be lifted from the heart of the race. Men and women are being crushed under needless regrets. And here is one of them: "Lord, if Thou hadst been here my brother had not died!" It was a regret that shut out the kindly light of the stars which God has ordained should shine and cheer us in our nights. I wish, therefore, to look at the incident with the utmost simplicity, in the prayerful hope that similar burdens may be lifted from the hearts of some who may read these words.

It was a beautiful friendship which united the Lord with the family at Bethany. Their home was very evidently one of His favourite resorts. He turned to it for its friendly peace. Perhaps He found in this little circle a love that was not tainted with interested ambition. Perhaps He found a friendship that sought no gift and coveted no place. Perhaps He found a full-orbed sympathy, unbroken by suspicion or reserve. Perhaps He found a confidence which was independent of the multitude, and which remained quietly steadfast whether He moved in public favour or in public contempt.

At any rate, Jesus was at home "in the house of Martha and Mary," and here all unnecessary reticence was changed into free and sunny communion. He loved to turn from the heated, feverish atmosphere of fickle crowds to the cool and restful constancy of these devoted friends. When the eyes of His enemies had been following Him with malicious purpose, it was spiritually recreating to look into eyes that were just quiet "homes of silent prayer." After the contentions of the Twelve, and their constant disputes as to who should be greatest, it was good to be in this retired home where friends found love's reward in love's sacrifices, and the joy of loving in the increased capacity to love. It is therefore no wonder to read, as we do so frequently, that "Jesus went out to Bethany."

And now a darker record begins. "A certain man was sick, Lazarus of Bethany, of the village of Mary and her sister Martha." We know. nothing about Lazarus, except that Jesus loved him. Not a single lineament of his character has been offered to our imagination. And yet, somehow, I feel as though I know him well. He was one of those glorious men about whom our modern Press could scarcely compose a single readable paragraph. He was a gracious, lovable nobody. He was a "home-bird." He was a lover of the fireside. He was a beautiful commonplace. He did nothing except live a noble life. He was one of the nobodies whose presence constitutes the very sanctity of home. And he was sick.

What will the sisters do? They know of the Saviour's mysterious power over sicknesses. They had heard of it; they had probably seen it. Should they send for Him? Lazarus would not hear of it! These good souls never will. Said Lazarus: "He has got something better to do than trouble about me. Trouble not the Master. Let Him go on telling His good news unto men." And the sisters heeded their brother. But he grew gradually weaker, and they took counsel together, perhaps unknown to their forbearing patient. And then a sort of compromise was born which paid respect to their brother's wish while giving expression to their own. "We won't exactly ask Him to come! We will just send Him the news and leave the decision to Him." "The sisters therefore sent unto Him saying, Lord, behold, he whom Thou lovest is sick."

What will the Master do? Surely He will haste with all speed to the stricken home! He will take comfort where He has so often received it. He will lift the burden where the burden has been so often lifted from Him. "When therefore Jesus heard that he was sick He abode at that time two days in the place where He was." It was one of those mysterious delays which so often burden our life. There were the sisters in Bethany, waiting, wondering, saddening. Will He never come? Has He forgotten? "Then after this He saith to the disciples, Let us go into Judaea again." And so He came to Bethany, but it was too late. Lazarus was dead.

"If Thou hadst been here! If only we had sent two days earlier! If only we had done it without consulting our brother! If--if--if only!" This is, I say, a type of needless regret. It was a retrospect which darkened sorrow. It added a deeper gloom to the night. And it was all so gratuitous, so needless, so unwise. Why should they now go back, and fetch remorse from yesterday, and load their heart to the point of bursting?

And the same remorseful "if" rankles in human life to-day. How often I have heard it when loved ones have been taken away. Poor laden hearts have added to their burden by their sharp regrets. "If we had only gone south instead of north." "If I had taken the first illness more seriously." "If I had only got her away when she began to grow tired." "If I had only given up that engagement." "If I had never gone away." "If we had called in the doctor earlier." And so the poor, weeping souls moan on as if our God was dead.

And how often I have heard the wail when some choice or enterprise has apparently failed. "If we had only put him into a trade instead of a profession!" "If only we had put him in a profession instead of a trade!" "If only we had never sent him away from home!" "If only we had taken the other alternative!" "If only we had listened to this man's counsel instead of that man's counsel!" "If only! If only!" Or perhaps there is some decision concerning ourselves about which we have now become uncertain when it is too late to make a change. We thought about it, we took counsel about it, we prayed about it. Then we acted, and now we think we see. "If only I had waited another week!" "If only I had taken the first post that offered!" "If only I had been contented with good instead of fondly looking for better!" And so there comes a seeming "after-wisdom." We assume that we are "wise after the event." Our lamp is now burning, but it has been kindled too late, and its only use is to reveal to us our tragic and irremediable mistakes.

Now in the case of Martha and Mary the remorseful regret was altogether needless. "If Thou hadst been here!" But He had been there all the time. He had been with them in deepest sympathy, in kindly thought, in gracious intention, in tender and yet ample plan. What they were thinking to be a lamentable mischance was a vital part of a larger scheme, begotten and inspired by unfailing love. They had scarcely, if ever, been out of His mind since He heard the news. There was no need for regret; everything was just . exactly right.

And so it is with most of the "ifs," the remorseful "ifs" that ravage and devastate our peace. If there be a personal devil, who makes it his work to sow seeds of unhappiness and discord and unrest, multitudes of these "ifs" must be of his unholy planting. And for this reason. They destroy filial trust; they destroy spiritual peace; they destroy the wide sweeping light of Christian hope. The devil sows these needless regrets, and the thorns choke the good seed, and our spiritual harvest is starved or destroyed.

And even supposing we have made mistakes, and we would dearly like to have the choice back again that we might take the other turning, what then? Who is our God? And what are His name and character? Cannot He knit up the ravelled bit of work, and in His own infinitely gracious way make it whole again? With all our mistakes we may throw ourselves upon His inexhaustible goodness, and say with St. Theresa, "Undertake Thou for me, O Lord."

It is the very gospel of His grace that He can repair the things that are broken. He can reset the joints of the bruised reed. He can restore the broken heart. He can deal with the broken vow. And if He can do all this, can He not deal with our mistakes? If unknowingly we went astray, and took the wrong turning, will not His infinite love correct our mistakes, and make the crooked straight?

XXIX. WISE FORGETFULNESS

IT was a wise and comprehensive prayer which the old saint offered when he said, "Lord, help us to remember what we ought not to forget, and to forget what we ought not to remember." Our memories are very defective, arid very erratic, and very unsanctified. Oliver Wendell Holmes said that "Memory is a crazy witch; she treasures bits of rags and straw, and throws her jewels out of the window." And memory remains capricious even when life has entered into the highest relations and has made a faith-covenant with the eternal God. We forget the way the Lord our God has led us. We forget all His benefits. We forget that we were "cleansed from our old sins." The remembrance of His mercy sometimes goes clean out of our mind. Memory has some very big holes, and some big things drop away into oblivion.

But just now I want to consider the other aspect of her vagaries, her careful hoarding of things which she ought to throw away, the diligent remembrance of things which ought to be forgotten. There are some things for which we need mnemonic aids; there are other things for which we require mnemonic an#230;sthetics. If at some times the memory needs refreshing, at other times there is dire need of spring cleaning when her rubbish can be swept away. The full sanctification of memory, while it will vitalize some relationships, will surely destroy the sensitiveness of others.

It would be a blessed thing if we could lose the remembrance of our injuries. For one thing, the sense of injury is aggravated by remembrance. A spark is fanned into a flame, and "behold how great a matter a little fire kindleth." And in that fire it is our own furniture which is consumed. Some very precious furnishings of the soul are burned to ruin: Self-reverence and self-control are destroyed. Gentleness and modesty wither away like the undergrowth in a forest fire. Indeed, every power in life is damaged, even conscience herself being seared. But apart from these moral damages, what an uncomfortable guest this is to entertain in one's remembrance!

She keeps us continually ruffled and feverish. She fills the chambers of the soul with heaviness and gloom. She despoils us of the sweet sunshine of grace, and she sours every feast. Why should we keep her? Above all, why should we give her so much attention? For when she absorbs the attention the Lord Himself is eclipsed. If this bitter resentment could just become incarnate, and in visible ugliness could sit with us at our table, we should very speedily order her out of the house. If memory could lose her we should have great gain. If only we could forget her we should more clearly remember the Lord.

And then some of us are unwisely remembering our forgotten sins. There is the sin of a far-off yesterday, of which we have repented, and which we have confessed, and which the gracious Lord has forgiven, and yet we turn to it again and again with heavy and unrelieved heart. We go back and dig it up again when the Lord Himself has buried it, and when over its grave He has planted fair heart's-ease and lilies of peace. If ever we do return to those fields of defeat we ought to pluck a little heart's-ease or bring back a lily with us, that we may testify that where sin abounded "grace doth much more abound." There ought to be no room in our memories for the heaviness of forgiven sin. "His banner over us is love," and that banner is waving over the entire realm of our yesterdays if we have sought His pardoning grace.

Some people carry too vivid a remembrance of their beneficiaries. They are continually rehearsing to themselves the detailed story of their benefactions. In memory they pass them from hand to hand and back again, letting their right hand know what their left hand doeth. They had much better forget them. It is spontaneity that gives our ministries their worth, and a spontaneous character quickly throws off the remembrance of past services. The well is ever bubbling up anew, and the waters of yesterday are forgotten. Yes, it is spontaneity that makes our services fresh and refreshing. But self-consciousness, especially when it wears the smile of self-satisfaction, seeks to win commendation and reward, and so its real beneficence is stricken at the heart. When we begin to gloat over our goodness men begin to see that it is a trick and they will know that it is not the fruit of the tree of life. "Take heed that ye do not your righteousness to be seen of men," and we surely may add "nor to be seen of self." Forget them!

I will mention one other matter where a defective memory would be for our good--the matter of past attainment. It is possible so to hug our past triumphs that we never get beyond them. We may so linger with our success that we become satisfied, and have no aspiration for anything beyond. And thus it is literally true that some men's chains are found in their achievements. They have sat down in their victories, and life's progressive march has ceased. It was surely on some such peril as this that the Apostle was looking when he proclaimed his strong and positive determination to forget "the things that are behind." He used the figure of the racer who had covered part of the course, but whose goal was yet ahead. And the racer would not permit himself to turn and gaze upon the ground already run, still less to sit down and contemplate it with satisfaction. He would forget his present attainments in the quest of something better beyond. But we are always in peril of stopping in the midst of the course and seeking attainment in partial triumph. We have had a good spurt; let that splendid spasm do for the race! Or to change my figure, we are satisfied to win a battle, and we become indifferent about the campaign. Our satisfactions are premature. We fondle what we have done, and we are drugged by our successes into degeneracy and retrogression. Our minds must be filled with the vision of the fields that are yet to be won. "Glories upon glories hath our God prepared." Let us feel the call and the allurement of the days before us, and press on to the apprehension of their hidden treasure.

The grace of God is our provision for the sanctification of the memory. Perilous remembrances will be avoided if we are possessed by "the grace of the Lord Jesus." His grace is a "savour of life unto life," but it is also "a savour of death unto death." It can put things to sleep that ought never to have awaked. Apart from the grace of the Lord we have no sufficient power to hallow the memory. Mere effort will not avail. It is conscious communion with the Lord that ultimately transforms the consciousness. It is by the fulness of His might that all the spaces of the soul become realms of beauty and dwelling-places of eternal truth.

XXX. PREJUDGING CHRIST

"DOTH our law judge a man except it first hear from himself, and know what he doeth? "But that is Christ's fate every day and all the days. He is judged from hearsay. Men will not come face to face with Him and "know what He doeth." In the days of His flesh the Pharisees judged Him by extraneous standards. What was His birthplace? "Out of Galilee ariseth no prophet." What were the range and quality of His rabbinical knowledge? What heed does He pay to the customary ritualistic practices? "He eateth with unwashed hands." "Thy disciples fast not." The ordinary habiliments of the popular sect were wanting, and, therefore, He was despised and rejected. And these are typical examples of the prejudices through which many men looked at the Lord. It is the characteristic of a prejudice that it is small and. yet it produces monstrous perversions. A tiny obliquity in a lens can make the outlook grotesque. A small prejudice can so distort our vision of the Master that "when we shall see Him there is no beauty that we shall desire Him."

And small prejudices lead to great misjudgments in our own day. A man's opinion about the Church is allowed to fashion his relationship to the Christ. Some professing Christian has broken his covenant and betrayed his Lord, and, therefore, the Lord Himself is forsaken. Or men recoil from some phrase in a credal statement of the faith, and they turn their back upon the Lord of life and glory. Through churchianity many men interpret Christianity, and it is difficult to get them to come with a "fresh eye" to the contemplation of Christ. "Doth our law judge any man before it hear him?" Most assuredly this is the prejudgment which many men call conviction.

What is the right way of judging the Christ? First of all, we must bring the right implements. We must consecrate to the quest the medium of a sensitive heart. It will not suffice that we spend a week in worldliness and sin and then set about to give an hour's consideration to the claims of the Lord. It will be impossible to see even a sunset truly on those terms. The

136

heart that is befouled by unclean living is in no condition to estimate aright the glory of the Lord.

And then, in the second place, we must bring an open mind. Every blind must be up and every window opened. We must be perfectly candid and sincere in our approach. It is not enough to have a clean lens on the telescope--we must take the cap off! A man must strenuously rid himself of all perverting prejudices and draw near to the Lord with a single desire to see Him as He is. And to this end we must, in the third place, bring an alert imagination. We cannot vividly realize a page of ordinary history if our imagination is dormant or dead. If we are to see the movement of a past day in all its life and colour our imagination must be awake and active. Now this is peculiarly true when we come to the story of our Lord. All our powers must be surrendered to the quest, and more especially this talent of the imagination by which we recover the vitalities of yesterday and realize them as though we were in the very movements to-day.

And with this equipment we must "hear Him." We must hear Him patiently and hear Him through. We must hear Him concerning God, concerning Himself, concerning ourselves and our brother. We must listen to Him as He speaks of life, and love, and duty, and death, and destiny. We must listen while He tells us what we are and what we may be, and by what ministries of grace the transformation can be effected. But we must also know "what He doeth." We must pass from His words to His deeds, from a quiet listening in the oratory to the contemplation of His doings in the laboratory of the great world. We must investigate His work upon others and see what He has done. For instance, we must look at the man whose river of life was like the flowings of a sewer and which is now cleansed and pure as crystal. We must regard the other man whose will was like a trembling reed, and which has been converted into a resoluteness like the strength of an iron pillar. We must study His work in the gay, fast woman of the world who has been transformed and transfigured into a strong and gracious saint. Yes, we must honestly "know what He doeth." And we shall not have gone far in the search before our souls begin to bow in that wonder which is the parent of love and praise.

But this is not enough. If we are to lay aside every prejudice, and all that has hindered a true and full knowledge of the Lord, we must investigate His work upon ourselves. That is to say, we must convert inquiry into experiment. I cannot understand men and women passing the years in wordy controversy concerning Christ and never submitting His claims and promises to the severe and serious test of personal experience. Surely it is one of the first marks of candour in all our relationships to the Christ, to see if His word works, and if by the fulfilment of His conditions we ourselves are brought into the promised possession of peace and joy. Let a man sit down to the New Testament. Let him with clean, sincere eyes search out the requisite conditions of a conscious relationship with the personal Power of the world. Let him, if need be, write them out, and set them before him. Let him make them his maxims for the government of his life by day and night. Let him make test if there is anything in them. Nay, rather let him test if there is anything in Him. Let him experiment for twelve months. Let him do it with humility and reverence, earnestly desiring to know the reality of things behind the veil, and he shall assuredly feel the presence and the power of the Eternal. What will happen? The miracle will happen which has been wrought in innumerable lives. The man's heart will begin to be purified. The man's mouth will begin to be cleansed. His eyes will begin to be radiant with vision. His sympathies will put on chivalry and the joy of sacrifice. He will know that his Redeemer liveth.

Surely this is the way of honest inquiry. Let not a man be made the slave of unillumined prejudice. Let him not govern his life by hearsay and rumour. Let him be content with nothing second-hand. Let him seek a first experience of the things of the Highest, and the Highest will not leave him in the lurch.

XXXI. RIVERS OF LIVING WATER

"HE that believeth on Me, from within him shall flow rivers of living water." The springs of life are found in faith. Vital belief in the Lord Jesus brings the soul into communion with fountains of vitality. "All my springs are in Thee." And we cannot have springs without streams. Fountains make rivers. When the Divine life possesses the soul, it flows over in gracious ministries among our fellow-men. The affluence becomes an influence imparting itself to others. "From within shall flow rivers." And what shall be the character of the river?

The life filled with the Spirit of God is a minister of vitality. Wherever the figure of the river is used in the Scriptures it always implies the carriage and the impartation of life. "The river of water of life." "Everything shall live whither the river cometh." Those who are in communion with the Holy Spirit are to be the antagonists of death, and are to convey the life-giving powers of the eternal God. First of all, they will vitalize dead organizations. There is nothing more burdensome than an organization bereft of life. There is nothing more inert than machinery divorced from energy. The Church is cumbered by dead and dormant institutions. Everywhere there is the incubus of institutionalism that has no inherent vitality. Now, the disciples of the Lord Jesus are to bring the needful life. Their influence is to be that of a river upon a mill-wheel. It changes the inactivity of death into beneficent motion, and things that were only impediments become ministers of progress.

And the disciples of Christ are also to vitalize dead dispositions. Everywhere in human life there are withered and withering things which need to be quickened. In some lives hopes are drooping like spring blossoms that have been nipped by the frost. In other lives desires are fading, and are like plants that are suffering from thirst. And, again, in other lives the affections are ailing, and their strength is lapsing into perilous weakness. If we could only look into the secret places of the souls of men, we should be amazed in how many lives there is the touch of death. Now, the friends of the Lord Jesus are to move about among these drooping people like "rivers of water of life." The withered heart is to be thrilled by our presence. The drooping faculty is to lift itself up in new strength, by reason of the influence of our lives. We are to be the ministers of a mysterious but most real vitality. There is a significant passage in the Book of Job, which always seems to me to lend itself to rich and far-reaching interpretations. "For there is hope of a tree, if it be cut down, that it will sprout again, and that the tender branch thereof will not cease. Though the root thereof wax old in the earth, and the stock thereof die in the ground, yet through the scent of water it will bud and bring forth boughs like a plant." The old stock withering in the ground scents the presence of the water, and is quickened into newness of life. And so is it to be in the life of man. When the river of water of life comes near to souls that are drooping in disquietude and defeat they are to become alive again and clothe themselves in strength and beauty.

But, in the second place, the life filled with the spirit of God is to be a minister of purity. It is "clear as crystal," and in all its movements it is the enemy of all defilement. I have watched a strong and impetuous stream, born after heavy rains, pouring its fulness into a stagnant pool which had become the home of corruption. In the energy of its presence the corruption was unloosed and carried away; until the pool was left clean and clear as a sea of glass. And such is to be the influence of the disciples of Christ upon the established corruption of our day. The glorious energies of a redeemed life are to be poured into the settled defilement, to stir up and release it, and to bear it entirely away. Imagine a half-dozen pure and strenuous moral rivers flowing strongly in every village in our land! Imagine ten thousand such rivers doing their purifying work in a great city! Think of such rivers moving in every human fellowship! I remember a town council which had come into the hands of men of common and questionable character, and the government of the town was becoming debased. And a number of men, in whom the Spirit dwelled mightily, and whose influence was like strong rivers, entered the council and made it clean. Who has not known a committee saved by the strength of one man's consecration? And this is suggestive of the possible influence of every life. If our souls, by faith in the Lord Christ, are in communion with the springs of life, then a river of pure and purifying influence will most assuredly flow in all our common intercourse.

And, thirdly, the life filled with the Spirit of God is a minister of refreshment. There are desert places in the life when the springs seem far away. I got a letter the other day, in which my correspondent described what he called "a dry sorrow." The sorrow was so intense that he had lost the power to weep. It was grief that could not find relief in tears. It was "a dry and thirsty land where no water is." And everybody is familiar with such experiences, either in his own life or in the lives of others. Now, what is needed in such drought is some refreshing river. The prophet Isaiah declares that the ideal man is like "a river of water in a dry place." He brings refreshment to the soul that is held in perilous dryness. And who is to bring this refreshment? It can only be brought by men and women who live at the springs, and whose very presence is "a river of water of life."

And, lastly, the life filled with the Holy Spirit is a minister of hilarity. What more fitting symbol of gladness can we find than a clear, bright stream, dancing and leaping in the sunshine? Just to look at it, just to listen to it, is to catch the contagion of its joyful movement. And "there is a river the streams whereof shall make glad the city of God." The river that takes its rise in heavenly places in Christ Jesus, that is born among the hills of grace, and. flows in the sunshine of the Eternal Love, is bound to be a minister of gladness and cheer. The desponding and the melancholy, and those whose faces are heavy with the gloom of fear, are to be heartened and cheered when the disciple of Christ draws near, for the life filled with the Spirit is like a dancing, joy-imparting, and beauty-creating stream. How near do we come to this ideal? Perhaps we can give cups of cold water. But is our life richer than this, and is it suggestive of music and dancing? Is there anything hilarious in its influence? Is there the touch of joy, the gladdening ministry of those whose wills are in harmony with the King?

So, perhaps, instead of singing "Like a mighty army moves the Church of God," it might be a healthier expression if we sang, "Like a mighty river moves the Church of God"; a river carrying vitality, purity, refreshment, and making the birds to sing in the trees that line its banks.

XXXII. OUTSIDE THE WALLS

IT is a healthy experience to find rare flowers beyond the limits of one's own jealously-guarded garden. It is especially healthy when we have assumed that all the seed was in our own basket. It is altogether good to be made to wonder at these exotics growing so naturally in their alien bed. Our Lord seemed to take exquisite delight in pointing them out, and in emphasizing the teaching that His garden stretched beyond the confines of all the walls that had been built by men. He would stop His disciples on one of these alien roads--roads which to them had no significance except barrenness and desolation--and He would draw their reluctant eyes to some lovely flower growing by the way. Again and again He points them out, beautiful things outside the official circle, sweet presences beyond the limits of the recognized compound. He loved to reveal the flowers growing outside the walls.

There were ten lepers, and all of them were healed by the Master, but only one returned to give thanks for his healing, "and he was a Samaritan." This fine flower of gratitude was found growing beyond the pale of exclusive and traditional privilege. It is like "a root out of a dry ground." But there it is. A fair and beautiful thing which refreshed the spirit of our Lord. And so it is to-day; this noble and graceful flower of gratitude may often be found growing in profusion outside the outermost walls of the Church. And so it is again that within the walls, amid rich conditions of soil and climate, you may sometimes seek for the flower in vain. There are lives which claim exalted heavenly relations, but they lack the grace of gratitude. There are many who cry, "God be merciful!" who never cry, "God be praised!" But the sweet song is often heard outside the walls, and the sweet singer has not built her nest near the recognized altars of the temple.

"And the barbarians showed us no common kindness." That was a beautiful flower to be found growing in the wild home of caprice and superstition. Indeed, can we find anywhere a more beautiful flower than kindness? Is there any flower more pleasant to look upon, more sweet in its fragrance, more arresting and welcome to the eyes of men? And it was the barbarians who grew it in no common fashion. But where is the kindness born? From whose seed does it spring, and in what soil is it grown? With what sort of light and rain is it nourished? These questions lead us away to the source of every beautiful thing, even to the Great God, who has all "strength and beauty in His sanctuary." If the barbarians showed no common kindness, then the sweet flowers had been grown from seeds wafted from the paradise of God. When we call things by their right names, kindness is one of the fruits of the Spirit, and so these barbarians were just a part of the garden of the Lord.

"I have not found so great faith, no, not in Israel." Here, again, is our Lord's delight in outside treasure. Here is a steady, steadfast, appropriating faith, liberating the divine and holy energies of healing, and yet the man in whom it dwells is not registered among "the favoured people of God." He is an outsider, an alien, remote from the privileged vantage-ground of sunshine and shower, and yet this strong, virile, oak-like faith is growing mightily in his soul. The Kingdom was wider than the visible Church. Some who were unregistered in the earthly lists of saints had "their names written in heaven." There were spiritual correspondences when there were no official wires. There was secret fellowship where there was no visible communion. And all this should be deeply heartening to our souls. The realm of the Spirit is bigger than we know. Our church rolls are not its measure. There are men and women of unconfessed relations who are at mighty grips with God. There is secret faith that has not yet found public confession. There are faithful souls who will never "follow with us," but who are busy "casting out devils in His name." They may keep their own way, but the Lord knows them, and He seals their faith with His grace and power. They are "outside the walls," but they are "in the Lord."

"Other sheep I have which are not of this fold." And yet we are so tempted to think that all His sheep are in our fold, and we look with sharp suspicion on those that are outside our walls. I do not say that we bluntly deny them a part in the Tender Shepherd's care, but there is a reluctance of recognition, a want of generous candour, a disposition to withhold the right names from things, which is painful evidence that we severely limit the Shepherd's fold. Let us test ourselves by our regard for the Roman Catholics. How about the sheep of that fold? Do we heartily recognize the close communion between these sheep and our Shepherd? Do we readily acknowledge our common fellowship in the Lord? Or are we rather inclined to regard them as "black sheep," shepherdless, or herded only by subtle and deceptive hirelings? "Them also I must bring." We urgently need this broader and deeper sense of communion. It is amazing how, with all our federations and alliances, the "fold" prejudices are so intense and vigorous. It may be that we take the "fold" spirit instead of the "flock" spirit into our alliances, and we preserve our bitter divisions in the midst of our apparent union. At any rate, there are deep denominational reluctances that would be burned out completely if we had more of the fire of the Holy Spirit, for concerning all such roots of bitterness "our God is a consuming fire."

It is thus a wise and holy practice to look outside our walls. It is well to cultivate a wide expectancy, and to keep vigilant eyes upon every road, if perchance we may see signs of the coming of the Lord. If we find the red flower of love, let us relate it to God, for God is love.

XXXIII. HONEST MORAL JUDGMENT

"BY their fruits ye shall know them." So that is to be the standard of judgment. We are not to be concerned with the label, but with the fruit. We are not to draw our conclusions from the florist's catalogue, but from the actual garden. Men are to be judged, not by their professions, but by their character, not by their theology, but by their life. That is a very simple and reasonable principle. We are to test things by their issues. We are to go into the orchard and taste the fruit.

But the Master's teaching goes further than this. He insists that we are to be perfectly honest with our findings. If we find grapes We are to infer a vine, and not to suggest they are the product of a thorn. If we come upon figs we are to infer a fig tree, and not to suspect that they were borne on a thistle. We are not to belie our moral intelligence. We are not to cheat our instincts. We are not to confuse our common-sense. When I see fine moral grapes I must not hesitate in my conclusion that they are significant of so much nature and force of the moral vine. If I come upon spiritual grapes I must not insinuate that the serpent was the gardener, and that he himself has produced them. Wherever I see true goodness I must infer God. Wherever I find noble spiritual fruit I am to reason that it is a fruit of the Spirit. I must not confuse myself by saying "thorns" when it is as clear as the morning that I have found a cluster of grapes, and I must not say "thistles" when I have discovered ripe, delicious figs.

Now there is a strange unwillingness to apply this principle. There is a hidden perversity in the mind and heart which turns us away from its simplicity. We are timid and hesitant and uncertain in our application. We see a grape, and we are half fearful it may have sprung from a thorn. We see a fig, and we are dubious whether it may not have sprung from a thistle. So we have confused our reason and abused our moral instincts. We have misinterpreted hopeful and helpful signs and presences. We have limited "the Holy One of Israel." We have seen noble deeds, and attributed them to an alien power. We have witnessed glorious ministries of emancipation, and we have said they were done by "Beelzebub, the Prince of devils."

I must fearlessly apply the principle to my own life. I go into my heart and find a strange, wild country. There are many things that are withered, things that are distorted, and things that are ugly. There are thoughts and purposes sharp and cruel as thorns, and idle thistles abound on every hand. But suppose I find a few grapes, one tiny cluster of grapes? Then I must be honest with myself and rigidly true. I must not throw them to the thorns and thistles. I will say to myself: "These are true grapes, and they betoken the presence of the True Vine; the vine nature is here, the vine force, the Living Vine, the Christ." I find in my soul hints and suggestions of a better and larger life. My self-made earthclouds sometimes part asunder for a moment, and there breaks upon my gaze the glory of the heavenly country. I cannot quite say how they come. Sometimes they come in the quietness of the night. Sometimes they come in the convulsion of circumstances. I have known them come at the suggestion of a passing face. No matter how they come, what shall I do with them when they appear? Let me not call them flares from the pit, false beacons kindled by the Devil. Let me rather attribute them to the Father of Lights, the King of Glory.

I find also in my soul some responsiveness to the "higher calling." Often when the gleam shines before me my heart goes out in earnest craving. Sometimes I have a hunger and a thirst for righteousness; desire is kindled, and I long to be clothed in the beauty on which I gaze. What then shall I call these things? Let me be just to myself, especially when I am tempted to think myself God-forsaken and God-ignored. Here is a holy desire; then I will call it a grape. I will not call it a thistledown. It is a fruit of the Vine, and the Lord is near. So will I reason concerning every gracious moment in my soul, just putting out tendrils toward the spiritual and the eternal. It may be only petty and poor, but if there be any achievement at all I will give it its right name. It may be that the grapes are not yet fully formed. They may be hard and green and sour. Still, they are imperfect grapes, and they are the fruit of the Vine, and for these I will thank and praise His grace.

For every virtue we possess,
And every conquest won,
And every thought of holiness
Are His and His alone.

I must firmly apply the same principle to others. When I see grapes growing in their lives, I must not attribute them to thorns or thistles. I must be honest and firm in my reasoning. I never glorify God when I refer His works to the Devil. I must apply the reasoning to the people who are outside all Churches. I must not be tempted to label everything thorns and thistles, as though the Lord had no dominion and no ministry outside ecclesiastical fields. Here, again, perfect honesty and perfect candour will do the best service to the Lord. And I must follow the reasoning in my conclusions about the worshippers in Churches other than mine. How suspicious we are! How ready we are to call grapes thorns when they grow in another denominational field! Even when graces are evident, our consent is frequently so qualified, so ungracious, so reluctant! We reluctantly attribute them to "uncovenanted mercies." The seeds have been carried by stray winds, and the raindrops were intended for other fields!

How grudging we often are in our recognition of the grapes that grow in the Episcopal Church, and still more of those that are found in the Roman Catholic Church! I know there has been much in our history to make us resentful, and to fill us with a hot contempt. But, however tempted we may be, we must not yield to the injustice of denying the real grapes, and labelling the whole field as the home of thorns and thistles. There are winsomely gracious things in their midst. There is saintly character, there is mystical insight, there are marvellous range and power, and tenderness of intercession. There is chivalrous and heroic consecration and service. The grapes are evident. Let us gladly attribute them to the blood of the vine.

If I thus apply the Master's principle, honestly, consistently, universally, what will the result be?

First of all, I shall have an enormously enlarged conception of the workings of the Lord. I shall realize that His spirit is present everywhere, knocking everywhere, and that "His train fills the temple." And, secondly, I shall have the energy of exhilarant hope. I shall know that I cannot begin and work anywhere where the Lord has not anticipated me and done preparatory work for my coming. "The fields are white already unto harvest." So life will become more reverent, as perception becomes more delicate, and it will thus be filled with the spirit of hopefulness and praise.

XXXIV. THE COMING OF THE KINGDOM

I WANT to lead the meditations of my readers to a very familiar supplication in the Lord's Prayer: "Thy will be done." And with what better comment upon the words can I begin than this from John Calvin: "The substance of the prayer is that God would enlighten the world by the light of His Word, would form the hearts of men by the influence of His Spirit, and would restore to order, by the gracious exercise of His power, all the disorder that exists in the world." John Calvin thus brings us to a very definite conception as to what the prayer implies. The Kingdom comes just as God's thought and Spirit become dominant--His grace pervading human affection, His counsel illumining human judgment, His purpose fashioning human desire, His will controlling human movement. The Kingdom comes when His throne is revered, and when "the Lamb which is in the midst of the throne" constrains our wills in glad and spontaneous obedience. The Kingdom comes just as human relationships are shaped and beautified by the character of God, His righteousness expressed in our rectitude, His grace flowering in our graciousness, and His love finding a witness in everything lovely and of good report. The Kingdom comes when the King is honoured and when His statutes become our songs.

We must offer the prayer as seers. Our souls must be possessed by the glorious vision of a world held in the majestic yet gracious sovereignty of God. The beautiful land must be ours in holy vision and dream. Even while we pray, the poet within us must be at work, that mystic architect and builder in the soul who completes his temples and palaces before the first material stone has been laid and before the first sod has been turned. It is characteristic of the poet that he abides in the vision of the finished city while yet there is only a shanty on the ground. He sees the shining minarets and towers while yet lot stands in the first rude clearing of the desert waste. He feels the quiet of the haven while he is in the midst of the stormy seas, and he hears the pipes of peace in the very clash and combat

150

of war. The poet's soul dwells not so much in the temple when it is building as in the temple built. He is the seer, he carries the vision, and he reveals to us the goal of life and love and duty.

Now, the manner of the poet has always been a manner of the true apostles and saints. They have borne in their souls the vision of the finished work. It was even so with the Master Himself. "I beheld Satan as the lightning fall from heaven." It was the vision of a triumph not yet fully accomplished. It was the manner of the Apostle Paul. He looked "not at the things which are seen, but at the things which are not seen." He pressed "toward the mark for the prize of the high calling." It was also the manner of the Apostle John. "I, John, saw the holy city, the new Jerusalem, coming down out of heaven from God." And yet when he had the vision of the city how little of the city had been built! In place of a spiritual Kingdom he was confronted by mighty Rome, with her diseased pomp, and her festering luxuriousness, and her callous sensationalism, and her brutal pride. Instead of a sovereign Jesus he was face to face with a triumphant Nero! And yet he carried the vision of the finished work, and he saw "a new heaven and a new earth."

And we also are to pray as seers, holding in our souls the vision of the perfected man, the perfected city, the perfected State. And I will give two reasons for this. First, there is always a peril of our forgetting the glory of the goal in the distractions of the immediate tasks. If we lose the vision, we spoil the task. If we lose the vision of the end, the means become enthroned as the end. "Coming to church" becomes the end instead of communion with God. And, secondly, we must pray as seers because of the vast inspiration which is born of the vision of finished achievement. We perhaps more readily see the operation of this principle in the contemplation of finished disaster. If a man keeps his eye steadily fixed on probable defeat he will squander his resources all along the road. To constantly anticipate defeat is to almost make certain of it. The anticipation of triumph is one of the secrets of victory. Now, this is a most important truth in Christian Science. Amid much which is erroneous and perilous and foolish it proclaims a vital truth. Christian Science counsels all its disciples to keep their minds fixed on finished achievement. If they want to possess or to recover health they must contemplate themselves in the possession of health. They must steadily foresee the condition at which they want to arrive. And the principle prevails in the highest sphere. When we pray for the coming of the Kingdom our souls must rest in the vision of a moral and spiritual glory of which that Kingdom consists. We must "see the holy city . . . coming down out of heaven from God." We must offer the prayer as seers.

And, secondly, we must offer the prayer as labourers. Perhaps I want a stronger word than that; crusaders might serve the purpose better. The seer mist be a soldier. The vision must get into the mind as thought, it must get into the soul as desire, it must get into the body as the energy of surrendered limbs. We must have vision, but we must not be visionaries; we must be suppliants, but not cloistered and seclusive. We must labour to build the Kingdom for which we pray. This was characteristic of the Apostle John. He was a seer, but he was also a soldier. "I, John, your brother, and companion in tribulation, was in the isle which is called Patmos, for the word of God and for the testimony of Jesus Christ." This is surely worth noting. The bright vision came to the captive; the place of travail became the very door of hope. A more radiant apprehension of the heavenly city was the reward of fidelity to truth. John laboured in the building of the city for which he prayed. And may we not reverently say that this was also true of the Master? He carried the holy vision and He laboured for its fulfilment. "My father worketh hitherto, and I work." "I must work the works of Him that sent Me."

And where shall we work for the building of the city? First, in our own calling. We must carry the vision there, and build a bit of the Kingdom in the sphere where we earn our daily bread. We must cherish the very highest ideal of our own vocation. We must set it in the light of the Kingdom. We must array it. in the colours of the Kingdom. We must depict it in the excellences of the Kingdom. And then we must set our idealized employment in its place, in the finished and perfected Kingdom of God. And then, in the second, place, we must hold ourselves sacredly responsible to the highest we have seen, and diligently, and if need be prayerfully, seek to incarnate it in a flesh-and-blood creation. We must hold fast to the ideal, and make it visible in work and in worker, in matter and in manner, and in every ministry of relation between ourselves and our fellow-men. Difficult? Of course it is difficult, but why are we men except to confront the difficult thing, and bend it in obeisance to a pure and sovereign will?

And what we are to do with our own calling we are to do with our wider vocations as corporate members of the city and the State. No one can worthily say "Thy Kingdom come" and give no consecrated strength to the travail that makes the Kingdom come. In every city there are many crooked things needing to be made straight. There are many bitter pools needing to be made sweet. There are many galling yokes waiting to be shared. There are little children needing guidance, there are old people needing heartening, there are captives craving freedom. Is it nothing to you, all ye that do pray, "Thy Kingdom come"? We must come as seers to the need, and give our blood to remove it.

And, lastly, we must offer the prayer as watchmen. We must watch for the coming of the Kingdom, and we must proclaim the breaking day. I think, perhaps, we say too much about the night and too little about the morning; too much about the fastnesses of darkness, or, at any rate, too little about the growing splendours of the day. I sometimes think we could do with a society whose one work should be to watch the dawn and record the signs of advancing day. Its glad and privileged duty would be to watch for signs of the Kingdom, and wherever they were visible to make them known. Its symbol would be the morning star, and its motto, "Say to them that are of a fearful heart, Be strong!" It would be a society of scouts for observing and recording sunbeams, and the members would engirdle the earth in quest of good news. Daily papers would be diligently searched, not for news of strife, but for the great and winsome things which tell that the Lord is marching on. And it is marvellous what we may find in one day's newspaper if we scour it for signs of the Kingdom. And this must be the zealous quest of the suppliants of the Kingdom. We must let people know that the Kingdom is coming, and we must give them the proofs. "O thou that tellest good tidings to Zion, get thee up into the high mountains. O thou that tellest good tidings to Jerusalem, lift up thy voice with strength, lift it up, be not afraid; say unto the cities of Judah, Behold your God."

XXXV. THE POWER OF THE HOLY SPIRIT

WHEN the apostles received the power of the Holy Spirit what difference did it make to them? What kind of dynamic does the Holy Spirit bring to men? What change takes place in the lives of men to-day when they become companions of the Holy Spirit? What infirmities do they leave behind? What new equipment do they gain? I turn to the records of apostolic life and I put my inquiries there. What happened to these men? What kind of power did they receive when they had received the Holy Spirit?

First of all, then, I find an extraordinary power of spiritual apprehension. I know not how to express what I see. The apostles have a certain powerful feeling for God. They have a keen spiritual sense which discerns the realities of the unseen. It is as though their souls have developed latent feelers for the Divine. If we compare their dulness in the earlier days before the Holy Spirit was received, with their alertness afterwards, we shall see that the difference is most marked. The Master Himself describes them as "slow of heart." Their perceptions are blunt. They are dull to catch the spiritual side of things. But now when we turn to the record in the Acts of the Apostles we find this powerful sense of the Divine presence. It is as though a man has been sitting in a room with another man, but was only dimly aware of his presence; and then there came to him a refinement of his senses, and he gained a perfect assurance and a vivid knowledge of the other's company. The spiritual senses of these men were awakened, and they became aware of the "all-aboutness" of God. They have an intimate power of correspondence with Him which makes the unseen Lord a most real and intimate friend. And along with this sense of the Divine presence there is a refined apprehension of the Divine will. Everywhere in the apostolic life there is a tender and refined correspondence with the mind of God. Everywhere communications are being made between the Divine and human, and the human is strongly apprehending the Divine.

Sentences like these abound everywhere: "The angel of the Lord said unto me"; "The Spirit said to Philip, Go near"; "And the Lord said to Ananias"; "The Spirit said unto Peter." There is everywhere this suggestion of an intimate walk and an intimate knowledge of God's will. Is not this a power to be coveted, and a power to be desired? And it is a power given by the baptism of the Holy Spirit.

I look again at the lives of these apostles, and I find them distinguished by magnificent force of character. In the early days they were timid, pliable, unfaithful. In supreme crises they deserted their Master and fled. They were as reeds shaken by the wind. The wind that blew upon them from the haunts of desolation, the keen, perilous winds of persecution, made these disciples bend before their blast. The men were negative, hesitant, uncertain, altogether lacking in persistent force. But now the timid and fearful have become positive and affirmative. There is nothing lax about them, nothing wavering, nothing yielding. Their characters have become strong, and steady, and effective. I say they have got force of character, and they have the two elements that are always found in forceful character: they have light and they have heat. They have light in the sense of clarity of purpose. Their outlook is not confused. Their aim is perfectly clear. If we watch them in the service of their Lord we find them never to be diverted from their track. "This one thing I do." They have this primary element in a forceful character, the clarity of an undivided aim. And the second element in a forceful character is heat, the fire of a quenchless enthusiasm. And they certainly had this fire in glorious strength and abundance. The Acts of the Apostles is a burning book. There is no cold or lukewarm patch from end to end. The disciples had been baptized with fire, with the holy, glowing enthusiasm caught from the altar of God. They had this central fire, from which every other purpose and faculty in the life gets its strength. This fire in the apostles' soul was like a furnace-fire in a great liner, which drives her through the tempests and through the envious and engulfing deep. Nothing could stop these men! Nothing could hinder their going! "We cannot but speak the things that we have seen and heard." "We must obey God rather than man." This strong imperative rings throughout all their doings and all their speech. They have heat, and they have light, because they were baptized by the power of the Holy Ghost.

And I look again into the lives of these men who had been redeemed by the power of the Holy Ghost, and I find the energies of a glorious optimism. There is no more buoyant and exhilarating book in the literature than the book of The Acts. If we sit down and read it at a sitting we shall feel something of the swift and hopeful pace of its movement. I do not know that in their earlier days we should have described the disciples as "children of light." They easily lost heart, and the cloudy days filled them with dismay. But now, after they have received the Holy Spirit, we find them facing a hostile world. They are face to face with obstructions, with persecutions, with threats of imprisonment and death. But nowhere do we find a desponding or a despairing note. Ever and everywhere they are optimists in spirit. And what is an optimist? He is a man who can scent the coming harvest when the snow is on the ground. He can "feel the days before him." He can live in the distant June in the dingy days of December. That is an optimist, a man who can believe in the best in the arrogant and aggressive presence of the worst. He can be imprisoned in the desolations of Patmos and yet can see "the Holy City, the New Jerusalem coming down out of heaven from God." He can look at a poor, wayward, sinful Samaritan woman whose life is scorched like a blasted heath, and He can say, "The fields are ripe already unto harvest." And this power of optimism is always operative in the apostolic life. I find it in the springiness of their soul. You cannot break their spirit. You cannot hold them down in dull despair. "They laid their hands on apostles and put them in the common prison." And what happened after that? The morning after their release I read, "They entered into the temple early in the morning and taught." And here is another part of the record: "When they had called the apostles, and had beaten them, they commanded that they should not speak in the name of Jesus, and let them go. And they departed from the presence of the council, rejoicing that they were counted worthy to suffer for His sake." These men could not be held down. The spirit of optimism was ever dominant.

And with their springiness there was a marvellous spirit of joy. Theirs was not a dull buoyancy, but a radiant and a singing one. "And they raised persecution against Paul and Barnabas, and expelled them out of their coasts; and the disciples were filled with joy and the Holy Ghost"! "And at midnight Paul and Silas sang praises unto God"! Is not this the very spirit of power? These men had spiritual springiness, spiritual delight, because they had the spirit of Christian optimism, and this power they received when the Holy Ghost came upon them.

Do we wonder, then, that men of this kind, so endowed, have the additional power of witnessing for the Lord Jesus Christ? They witness by the arresting magnetism of their own transfigured character. They witness by their clear and enlightened apprehension of the Gospel by which they have been redeemed. And they witness by the grip of their words; words which were vitalized by the indwelling spirit of God. And we, too, shall receive a similar power when the Holy Spirit comes upon us. The same power is offered to us, to fit us for our condition, to equip us for our life. And what are the terms on which that power is received? They are these: that we are willing to offer our life for God, that the offer be made in all sincerity, made in simplicity, made in humble trust upon the Lord Jesus Christ. It means that we are willing to give up our sins, to lay down our pride. It means that we are willing to receive the Lord as our guest, and to allow Him to rule and to dominate our lives.

XXXVI. KEEPING THE ROADS OPEN!

"IF thy brother sin." But we must be quite sure about it. We can so easily be mistaken. Summary judgment can be villainously unjust. The assumed criminal may be altogether innocent, and his supposed crime may be the ugly figment of our own diseased imagination. For through what perverting media we can look at one another, and what monsters we appear when seen through a distorting lens! And therefore the primary rule of guidance in all presumed offences is that a man should examine his lens. Is the lens a perverting medium? Am I looking through a magnifying glass, and therefore magnifying trifles? Is the whole matter an exaggeration? And is the real fault in my own eye? Let me not leap to conclusions concerning my brother. "Let every man be swift to hear, slow to speak, slow to wrath."

But assuming that there is no distorting lens corrupting our judgment, and that the offence is palpable when seen through cool and simple sight, what then should be our course? "Rebuke him." Well, that would be pleasant enough. It is an exercise which provides a feast for the majority of people, and we set about it with rare satisfaction. But there are rebukes and rebukes. There is a rebuke which is only intended to satisfy the offended, and there is a rebuke which is purposed to rectify the offender. A legitimate rebuke is more than a vent for passion--it is a minister of redemption. It is intended to do more than work off my spleen; it is purposed to remove my brother's defilement. It is to be used not so much for the relief of my wound, but for the healing of his. The wound of the offended is clean, and time will most surely heal it. But the wound of the offender is unclean, and it may easily fester into something worse. And therefore I say the primary purpose of a rebuke is not to gratify my temper, but to help my brother to recover his broken health.

Now, we may quite easily ascertain whether our rebuke has been of the kind counselled by the Master, a medicated kind, and the test is to be found in whether we are prepared to go further with our Lord. "If he repent, forgive him." If our rebuke has been healthy and wholesome, we shall be quite ready to take the further step as soon as occasion offers. The fine aim and trend of all Christian rebuke is ultimate reconciliation. A rebuke is not an instrument of punishment; it is an instrument of adjustment. It is not penal, but surgical, and always and everywhere it is purposed to be a minister of moral and spiritual restoration. To put the matter in a word, in all the offences we suffer, our after-conduct should seek the moral recovery of the offender.

Now, let us seek to grasp one or two vital principles which lie behind this teaching. And I think we must begin here: a man's finest asset is his integrity. It is just as well that even so familiar a commonplace as this should be re-emphasized. We are in such general agreement about it that it is apt to be ignored. Let a man destroy his integrity, and he destroys the finest jewel in his life. "A man's life consisteth not in the abundance of things which he possesseth." Things provide only an existence; in character is found the life.

And the second step is this: the finest contribution which any man can make to a city or a nation is the contribution of an unblemished character, the gift of a scrupulously clean and consistent life. It is ever a temptation to men to esteem gifts more than dispositions, to exalt the showy and the dazzling more than the inherently good. We are captured and fascinated by genius, and talent, and cleverness, and subtle and ingenious accomplishments. And yet these do not constitute the sterling wealth of the corporate life. When a man has given only brilliant genius to his country he has not given his best. The best we can give is not our interest, not our service, but a chivalrous character, massive and undefiled.

If, therefore, a man has lapsed from moral and spiritual health, and is squandering his finest treasure, it should surely be his brother's concern, for his own sake as well as for the sake of the offender, to keep the way open for his return. It is wise, even for our own sakes, to seek an offender's restoration. When a man becomes morally defiled he introduces uncleanness into the commonwealth. Our sense of the corporate life is so dull and faint that we only very imperfectly discern the influence of the part upon the whole. Our conception of society is mechanical, not organic; it is political, not vital. We think of society as a chance collection, not as a nerve-pervaded corporation. At the best we regard it only as an aggregation and not a union. But the teaching of the Scriptures brings before us a far more profound conception. According to the New Testament, society is not a mere combination, like a heap of miscellaneous articles which the ocean has thrown up on the shore. The race of men constitute one vast, nervy body, with all the members vitally interdependent, vitally intercommunicative, inherently one and whole, every part related to every other part in community of interest, and every part suffering in so far as any part is undeveloped or bruised or broken. Let me state quite boldly the implications of this teaching. So long as China's hordes are stagnant we ourselves will remain immature! So long as the cannibal tribes of tropical islands drowse on in their animalism we ourselves will not be fully awake! So long as anywhere in broad England any man is mentally or morally dwarfed, every other man will be hindered from gaining his appointed stature! No man will walk at his full height so long as any man remains a pigmy! One moral cripple affects the pace of the race! And therefore if a man "goes wrong," if he becomes morally filthy, whether in slum or suburb, there is no isolation-hospital in which his nefarious influence can be safely confined. Prison-walls may isolate bodies, they cannot destroy the nerve communications of the race. We are every man and woman the poorer for every man and woman in gaol to-day.

If, therefore, my brother sin, what shall I do? Why, for the sake of everybody, try to get him right again. To rebuke him is not enough; to punish him unduly may aggravate the danger. The only adequate purpose is to get him whole again. And therefore did I say it is for the offended to keep the road open for the offender's return.

Now, according to the teachings of the Master, one of the methods for keeping open roads in the moral and spiritual realm is the ministry of forgiveness. "Forgive him." Yes, but the word is not used with the thin significance of effeminate emotion. The forgiveness of the New Testament is not emotional, but motional; not pathetic, but energetic; not a matter of cheap tears, but of sacrificial service. It is more than pardon, it is chivalry. It is more than the withdrawal, of the sword, it is the conversion of the sword into a ploughshare. It is the destructive transformed into the constructive and employed in positive culture. It is no use-considering anything else than this when we are thinking or speaking about forgiveness. There are many counterfeits about; masquerading as forgiveness, but they have no vital kinship with reality. There is a superciliousness which patronizingly utters sacred words, but its poverty is exposed by its very pride. Forgiveness is not a passive acquittal; it expresses itself in the ministry of self-sacrificing toil. And such a spirit, by the teaching of the Master, will assuredly keep the road open for a sinful brother's return, and we shall be called "the repairers of the breach, the restorers of paths to dwell in."

But a disposition of this kind demands that .we ourselves have faith in the spiritualities. Practical materialists will have no concern for these things, because the currents and forces in which they believe are of an altogether mundane kind. It is needful to have a firm conviction of the reality of the spiritualities, and of their power to strengthen or corrode the temporalities which are often so glaringly showy and so superficially majestic. If we are to exercise the ministry of forgiveness, in the way in which I have indicated, it is needful that we believe in God, and in the energies of godliness, and in our own possible co-operation in the ministries of redemption. And, therefore, how fitting was the prayer of the apostles which succeeded this high counsel of our Lord, "Increase our faith"!

XXXVII. A FRIEND OF THE SUSPECTED

SUCH was the character of the Apostle Barnabas. From his life there emanated the strength and perfume of goodness, and he ministered among his brethren as the son of consolation. Whenever people were under a cloud he brought the light of cheer. Whenever they moved in timidity, by reason of suspicion, he brought the atmosphere of confidence. I want to look at his character and inspect the springs of his disposition and service.

How was his life related to God? First of all we are told he was "full of faith." The word "full" is strangely significant. There are analogies which may help us in our apprehension of this side of his character. We speak sometimes of a singer as being "full of music." I spent an hour a little time ago in the presence of a distinguished singer. Every moment she seemed to be bubbling over with song. Every interest in her life was controlled by the dominant passion. Every power in her being seemed to sway to one inspiration like fern and reeds responding to the common movement of the wind. An organist's fingers are raining music even when he is not at the organ. They are moving to inaudible sounds. The soul that is full of music brings its music into everything, and every circumstance becomes the home of song. And so it is with the life that is "full of faith." Let me give another analogy. When the conductor of an orchestra raises his baton the eyes of every instrumentalist are fixed upon him. It would be right to say that the orchestra is "full of obedience." Every member in the fellowship is controlled by one will, and all the powers co-operate in this common subjection. The life that is "full of faith" is a life in which every power of the soul pays homage to the will of the Lord. Every faculty is open in trustful dependence on the Unseen, and this obeisance is paid in all the varying circumstances of the ever-changing road. Barnabas was "full of faith."

And the second characteristic of his supreme relationships was this: he was "full of the Holy Spirit." This fulness is a sequent to the other. Faith is the willingness of the soul to receive the Holy Spirit. Faith implies that the soul is disposed to Divine hospitality. It is willing to entertain the Lord. It is ready to open the door to heavenly presences, and to throw the windows open to heavenly airs. I suppose that some of the most nauseous places on the face of the earth are on the high seas. Where the air is purest and cleanest uncleanness may most abound. There can be nothing more repulsive than the air of many a sailor's cabin, and this in spite of the fact that his boat is enveloped in the purest air that enswathes the earth. We can breathe a stenchful atmosphere when immeasurable leagues of finest air are pressing round on every side. Now, to open the port-hole is to have fellowship with the infinite. The little cabin becomes filled with air that has been washed and sweetened by the influences of immeasurable space. And so it is that faith opens the life to breathings of the Infinite Spirit. Faith makes the soul competent to receive the Holy Spirit. Barnabas was open to the Divine, and the Divine became his guest.

Now turn to his human relationships. What should we expect such a man to be in his active life in the world? I should venture to characterize the life of this early apostle in one phrase. He was the friend of the suspected. First of all he was the friend of suspected individuals. Saul heard the call of his Lord, and responded, and became a disciple of the Son of God. Now, there is always a strange reluctance to believe in the goodness of people who have been reclaimed. We suspect that their apparent improvement may be only a fresh disguise of their vice. Their tears may be only part of their trickery. We say to ourselves and to one another, "We have known him of old." Or we say, "What is he up to now?" His conversion is regarded as a new make-up by an old actor. In some such way was the Apostle Paul regarded at his conversion. He was the object of deep suspicion. He was suspected of being a Jesuit before even Jesuitry was born. He might be seeking deeper intimacies in order that he might carry out malicious designs. "They were afraid, and did not believe that he was a disciple." What then can be done for a man who is treated with such chilling vigilance? "Barnabas took him and brought him to the apostles." It was a very delicate companionship which Barnabas thus offered to the timid convert to help him along the early steps of the way. I try to imagine the two as they made their way to the apostles' company. I try to imagine the character of their intercourse. I can feel how they would grow into each other, and how heart and mind would commune with heart and mind in a fellowship never to be broken. And this is the kind of strengthening communion which thousands of converts need in our own day, especially those who are leaving behind them the record of glaring and notorious lives. They need the friendship of men who shield them from suspicion, and who by their confidence nourish their frailty into hopeful strength.

Let me give another instance of this man's disposition and service. We lose sight of the convert Saul. He became a recluse. He retires into comparative privacy and solitude. He seems to be lost to the Church, and no one appears concerned about his whereabouts. For some years he vanishes from our sight. And then Barnabas came to Antioch to execute a commission with which he had been entrusted by the Church in Jerusalem. And when his task was done he "departed to Tarsus to seek Saul." I like to think of that man setting out on his journey in quest of the other man destined to be the great apostle to the Gentiles. It seems as though the Apostle Paul was twice saved by Barnabas to the services of the Christian Church. He brought him to Antioch, and the great missionary crusade began. How much we are indebted to the folk who seek out the hidden people, the folk who fetch us out of our holes! There are thousands of people hiding away in forgotten corners, and Barnabas is needed to bring them to their places of ministry and service.

There is one other instance where Barnabas overwhelmed the suspicions of others and redeemed the defeated man from alienation. John Mark had become fearful. He was perhaps afraid of the fever that haunted the swamps along the Asiatic coast. Or perhaps it was the looming of other kinds of danger and difficulty. Whatever it was it was something that frowned upon them, and Mark left the apostolic company and turned back. He at once became a child of suspicion. And at a later day, when a new enterprise was being commenced, "Paul thought not good to take him." But again Barnabas interposed and "took Mark." How much we are indebted to the gracious folk who are willing to give us a second chance! What a radiant record shines behind the names of those who have permitted the fallen to try again! It is the way of the Lord.

When Jonah had rejected his first command, and had turned his back upon it, and wandered in the ways of trespass and transgression, the Lord gave him a second chance. "And the word of the Lord came to Jonah a second time." This is the disposition that needs to be manifested by the followers of the Christ. There are multitudes of people who have broken their covenant, who have deserted to the foe, who have eaten the bread of the enemy, but who are longing to return to the old camp. Barnabas was the friend of just such longing souls. He was the helper of those who had failed. He was the advocate of the second chance.

But he was not only the friend of suspected individuals. He was the guardian of suspected causes. There were strange doings at Antioch, which were reported to Jerusalem as the extension of the Kingdom of God. Great doubts arose as to its being genuine, and many looked upon it with severe suspicion. Barnabas was sent as a deputation of inquiry. And what is the record of the mission? "When he had seen the grace of God," Barnabas had the requisite light. His eyes were anointed with eye salve and his perceptions were clean and clear. He knew the old fruit, even when he found it growing in a new garden. He recognized the old tokens of grace, even when they were revealed in strange conditions. "When he had seen it he was glad." And these, too, are the folk we want in our own time. We need people who can see Christ when He appears in a new dress, who can discern the cause of the Kingdom when it shows itself in novel conditions. We need the spirit of candour and of consecrated expectancy, and for these we require the fulness of faith and the indwelling presence of the Holy Spirit. There is great work for Barnabas nowadays, for everywhere God is revealing Himself in new and diverse manners, and watchful, faithful men will love His appearing.

XXXVIII. THE HIGHER MINISTRIES OF HOLIDAYS

WHY did our Lord go "every night" into the mountain? And why was it His custom to walk so frequently in the garden? It was because He felt the boon companionship of Nature, the friendly helpfulness of the vast and the beautiful. Mountain and garden were allies of the spirit, silent Greathearts who ministered to Him in the pilgrim way. He sought the mountain when He was pondering over great decisions. He was found in a garden "in the night in which He was betrayed." He heard wondrous messages in her voices; in her silences, too. He listened to mysterious speech. He read the evangel of the lilies. He understood the language of the birds. He read the face of the sky. He shared the secrets of the soil and the seed. He walked through the cornfields on the Sabbath day, and the ears of corn ministered to a richer Sabbatic peace. He stooped to hold intercourse with the grass of the field. The wind brought Him tidings of other worlds. The vineyards gave Him more than grapes and wine; they refreshed and strengthened His soul. Everywhere and always our Saviour was in communion with His willing and immediate friends in the natural world. Nature was to Jesus a blessed colleague in the soul's commerce and fellowship with the Highest.

And we, too, seek rest and recreation by the seashore or countryside. Our bodies become like lamps that are in need of oil; they burn a little dim and uncertain; and sometimes because we are a little spent and weary we become very unpleasant to other people, like lamps that have begun to smoke. We are consuming wick rather than oil, and it is attended with offensive consequences all round. And so we must get our lamps refilled, and we find the precious oil in the green pastures or by the deep-sounding sea.

Now, it is good for us to remember that a jaded body can be greatly helped through the ministry of a refreshed mind. A noble thought in the mind has ennerving communion with the entire circle of our life. And the principle is even still more deep and certain in its influences when for a noble thought we substitute an exuberant soul. "Thy faith hath saved thee," said the Master, and the extraordinary physical convalescence was directly related to a mood and disposition of the soul. And, therefore, although we may get valuable stock of oil for our spent and sputtering lamp by just lying down on the slopes of the hills, or throwing ourselves on the sands, yet the filling would be greatly helped if to a prudent physical indolence we added refined and noble thought. Golfing will be all the more effective as a tonic if a man is open to the Divine. We cannot get the best out of Nature if we are closed against her deepest secret. We may depend upon it that when Jesus prayed upon the mountain He got the very best that the mountain had to give. When He knelt in the garden of Gethsemane the olive groves contributed far more than restful shade and perfume. Our bodies draw upon Nature's finest essence when our spirits are in communion with Nature's God. And so in all our thinkings about rejuvenation let us include the interests of the spirit. The most refreshing holiday is that which is pervaded by an abiding communion with God. Our spiritual habits are the ministers or the masters of our bodies, and we do a very ill turn to our tired bodies if, by the manner of our holiday, we choke the channels of the highest life.

I know that Nature has frequently an unconscious and a very blessed influence upon our minds and souls. A revelation of vastitude may have a most expansive influence upon us, even if the Divine do not consciously possess our thoughts. The bounding wave may give us a very exhilarating influence, and so may the jocund daffodils, or the bright loneliness of the uplifted hills. Nature may soothe us, or she may excite us; she may be a stimulant or a sedative. But this unconscious influence is by no means sure. If the presence of broad spaces and towering heights were always ministers of expansion how do we explain those multitudes in our rural population whose minds are small, and dull, and unresponsive, and who have no conscious or unconscious communion with the subtle beauty or the far-stretching glory of their surroundings?

But why go to a farm labourer for our example? We may find the witness in our own experience. We have often been to the royal seats of Nature's majesty or beauty, we have climbed her awful mountains, we have walked her broad domains, we have sailed her immeasurable seas, and in very truth we have returned home as small as we went away. The body has gained something, but not the mind or the soul, and, because the mind and the soul have been locked up like the rooms we have left behind in the city, our very bodies have not recovered that exuberant strength which was intended for them in the gracious purpose of God.

In all our holiday-making let us deliberately commune with the Divine. I am painfully aware that the very form of the phrase I have used is suggestive of a task, and appears to be uncongenial to the holiday mood. But there can be nothing in all our plans more holiday-like and more holiday-giving than just this simple purpose to commune with God. Does it stint our holiday feeling to recall the face and the tenderness of our little child? When we are in some almost awful splendour, is the thought of love an intrusion which darkens the privilege into task? Surely the thought of the beloved deepens and chastens the joy! And so is it in the highest realms and reaches of thought; the right thought of God deepens and enriches the holiday mood and puts us into communion with the very springs of life and joy and peace. We are going back to the old place, on the hill, on the moor, or by the sea. Have we ever met the Lord there? Have we ever seen the mystic cloud upon the hills? Have we ever seen Him come walking on the waters? Have we ever felt His Presence in the cornfields? Has He ever talked with us as we stooped to pick a flower by the way? Never met Him? Ah! then, we don't yet know our holiday place as we may know it, and as, please God! we may know it before we come back home again. We have only seen it in the light of common day. Wait until we have seen it in His blessed fellowship and we shall be amazed at the glory! We have seen the common bush and we think it wonderful; wait until we have seen the bush burn with the radiant Presence of God. Wait until we have been up the hill with the Lord, and in. the far-reaching glory He has become transfigured before us. The sense of His Presence never spoils our freedom or chills our pleasure; it adds sunshine to light and delightful music to all our songs. When He walks with us as we journey to Emmaus He opens up everything.

What, then, shall we do on our holiday? First of all, let us quietly cultivate the sense of the Presence of our Lord. Let there be no stress about it and no strain; the quieter it is, the more natural and familiar, the better it will be. All that we need to do is just to call Him to mind and to link Him with the beauty of the glory we contemplate. Call Him into your mind as freely and as naturally as you would recall the thought of a loved one whom you have temporarily forgotten. You are climbing the slope of some glorious hill, or you stand upon its shoulder or its summit; quietly call to your mind: "The strength of the hills is His also." "Who by His strength setteth fast the mountains, being girded with power." "Faith has still its Olivet and love its Galilee." Or you are walking by the shores of the incoming sea: "The sea is His and He made it." "There's a wideness in God's mercy like the wideness of the sea." Or you are gazing upon the wonders of sunrise and sunset, upon their gorgeous harmony of colours, upon the mighty architecture of embattled clouds: "He clothed Himself in light as with a garment." "The heavens declare the glory of God, and the firmament sheweth His handiwork." "The Sun of Righteousness shall arise with healing on His wings." Or you are swept by the fresh, health-giving wind, from the deep, or on the heights: "He rideth upon the wings of the wind."

Thy bountiful care,

What tongue can relate,

It breathes in the air.

"And He breathed upon them and said, Receive ye the Holy Ghost." Or you are amid the perfumed loveliness of the flowers of the field:

Thy sweetness hath betrayed Thee, Lord;

Dear Spirit, it is Thou!

Would this gentle recollection interfere with the holiday? Would it impoverish it? Would it chill it? Or would it not rather warm and enlarge it, making every avenue bright and luminous, changing commandments into beatitudes:

And our lives would be all sunshine

In the sweetness of our Lord.

"Thou shalt remember the Lord thy God," and His statutes shall become thy songs.

And then I would give a second counsel. Let us seek the mystic mind of God in the creations of the natural world. For these material presences are speaking to us. They are the wonderful shrines in which are to be found still more wonderful messages. Do not let us confine our wonder to the shrine and ignore the message. Let us hold ourselves receptive to the secret, spiritual thing. Our Saviour elicited the secret of the lilies. He read an evangel as He saw the birds on the wing or in their nests. Everything was to Him a kind of envelope, and He reverently opened it and found the mystic scroll. And so was it with the psalmists and the prophets. Material things were the bearers of spiritual things, and these old seers continually gather the secret treasure. Charles Kingsley said that whenever he went down a country lane he felt as though everything about him, every leaf, and bud, and flower, were saying something to him, and he was pained by the feeling of his density. But he heard many, many things, and he has told them again to us. And in our own degree we all may do it. At any rate, we can question these sublime and beautiful things, and rightly to ask a question is to put oneself in the mood for receiving a reply. Why not begin with a flower? "What message hast thou here for me, thou tender, beautiful, gracious thing? What tidings dost thou bring?" Maybe not all at once will our spirit discover the answer, but it will not be long before we are sensitive enough to catch some whisper from our God. Material presences, continually wooed by the spirit, will yield their spiritual treasure, and the jubilant heart will store up its growing wealth of grace. And so, I say, cannot we quietly interrogate our surroundings, without fuss or obtrusion, and by wise questioning prepare ourselves for great replies? "What hast thou to say to me, O breaking wave, the lifted hill, flying cloud, gentle breeze, or roaring blast?" And if some day our holiday plans are broken by the broken weather it will be a blessed thing to consult the falling rain, and ask what secret messages it may have for men, and what news it brings of things Divine! These are simplicities, but they will lead us into profundities, and without any weight or burdensomeness they will keep our souls "alive unto God."

What sweetness on Thine earth doth dwell!

How precious, Lord, these gifts of Thine!

Yet sweeter messages they tell,

These earnests of delight Divine.

These odours blest, these gracious flowers,

These sweet sounds that around us rise,

Give tidings of the heavenly bowers,

Prelude the angelic harmonies.

And thus let us imitate the Scriptures in regarding the ministries of Nature as illustrative of the ministries of grace. While we look at the seen, let us also look at the unseen. Let the symbol become a veil through which we can see Him "who is invisible." Let us use our happy surroundings as modes of expression between God and the soul, and the soul and God.

Such communings do not detract from the worth and wealth of a holiday, they rather enrich and augment it. They give freedom and height and expansion to the soul; and high spirits are good spirits, and good spirits are the very first essential to bodily health and exuberance. To "sit in heavenly places in Christ Jesus" makes one akin to the secret power which dwells in the blowing corn and the rolling wave.

We do not need to have vast panoramas, or gigantic mountains, or immeasurable seas, before we can enter into sacred communion with the spirit of Nature. We can begin at home in more limited surroundings. We have always with us the pageant of the clouds. We have the wonder of the sky. "The noblest scenes of the earth can be seen and known but by few; it is not intended that man should live always in the midst of them; he injures them by his presence, he ceases to feel them if he is always with them; but the sky is for all . . . fitted in all its functions for the perpetual comfort and exulting of the heart,--for soothing it, and purifying it from its dross and dust." We have always, not far away, the treasures of the gardens and the flowers of the fields. We have the birds, and our Lord found a great evangel in the sparrows! Yes, it is altogether true what Stevenson said: "The spirit of delight comes often on small wings." Let us watch the commonplaces in Nature. We shall find them vistas opening into the infinite and eternal. "The earth is the Lord's and the fulness thereof, the world and they that dwell therein." "Holy, holy, holy, is the Lord. The fulness of the whole earth is His glory."

JOHN H. JOWETT

Look For Other Books Published By:

Classic Domain Publishing

NOTE: The books from *Classic Domain Publishing* are intended to awaken people — Christians, Backsliders, and Non-Christians alike - to the urgency of seeking Christ in order to make the rapture or to make it to heaven if they should die before the rapture. Most of the books by *Classic Domain Publishing* are Public Domain and are "re-published" in order to make the books more readily available to the modern era in the *"Last Minutes"* of these *"Last Days."*

If there are other Public Domain books that have changed your life, please let me know so that we can perhaps list it or publish it as a "life changing" book.

Contact me by email at:

peralta_mike@hotmail.com

Other Life Changing Works

(List below by Mike Peralta – Chief Editor of Classic Domain Publishing)

The Bible both Old and New Testament. The best book as God never lies and He is never mistaken.

"Hell Testimonies" by Mike Peralta. This is a compilation of several Hell Testimonies from several people around the world. In my opinion this is the best book, after the Bible, (not because I'm the author) but because it mentions many types of sins that will send you to Hell. Some of the sins mentioned will probably hit home to you as you read this book. This book has helped me truly repent of sin more than any other book.

"While Out Of My Body I Saw God, Hell, and the Living Dead" by Dr. Roger Mills. This is a superb book about Hell. Jesus explains some things about Hell and sin that I have never read anywhere else. However, as far as I can see, it is all consistent with what the bible says.

"A Divine Revelation of Hell" by Mary Kathryn Baxter. This book shows in graphic detail what torment people in Hell are suffering. This book has been read by many and has helped many repent from their sins and obey God in their lives.

"Heaven Is So Real" by Choo Thomas. This book discusses both Heaven and Hell and reveals a great deal about the love and personality that Jesus has to His children as evidenced by how Jesus interacts with Choo Thomas. With a tenderness and friendly and loving and compassionate heart, you will learn the character and demeanor of Jesus through this book.

"Backsliding to Hell" by Mike Peralta. This book is written to help the backslider or those who are sinning after receiving Jesus in the past. It clearly explains through the Bible that the backslider will definitely go to Hell unless he or she repents of their sinning and turns back to Jesus. At first, to avoid promoting myself, I was not going to include this in my list of life changing books (truth2.weebly.com) but the Holy Spirit insisted that I include this book, so it must be even more important than I, myself, realize.

Rapture and Tribulation books by Susan Davis: "Bride of Christ Prepare Now", "Left Behind After The Rapture", "Rapture or Tribulation", "Marriage Supper of the Lamb", "I Am Coming (Volumes 1 to 6)" by Susan Davis and Sabrina De Muynck. These rapture books are prophetic messages from Jesus to help prepare the Bride of Christ (Christ's true church) on how to prepare for the very soon rapture. It clearly shows that those who are not ready and are not looking to Jesus' soon coming will be left behind to face the anti-christ and certain death at the hands of the most ruthless evil dictator that will take power and world domination after the rapture. Also near the time of the rapture there will many deaths and those who are not ready will end up in Hell.

"Final Call, Exodus, My Son David, True Maturity" by Deborah Melissa Moller (Four Book Series). This four part series (combined in one book) has helped me more than any other book to get close to Jesus and obey God's will. It is like Jesus is personally teaching me how to follow Him, obey Him, love Him, and to do the Father's will. This is an extremely valuable book. It is truly a *Pearl of Great Price*. It is provided by Jesus to prepare His Bride for the very soon rapture.

Links to rapture books are also at: truth2.weebly.com

I urge you to read all these books — especially the Bible — over and over again. There is extremely little time left to get right with God. Jesus is returning much sooner than you think and there is soon to be terrible judgments on earth.

Surrender your life completely to Jesus now.

It is extremely and eternally dangerous to delay your full and absolute commitment to Christ. It doesn't matter what anyone else tells you — they cannot help you when you end up in Hell. Trust only God. Of course, love and pray for everyone — but trust only God.

Seek Him with all your being now before it's too late.

Feel free to email me at:

peralta_mike@hotmail.com

Made in the USA
Middletown, DE
15 November 2022

15111814R00099